No Business as Usual

No Business as Usual

Sermons for the Lectionary, Year A,
Pentecost through Christ the King

BRUCE L. TAYLOR

WIPF & STOCK · Eugene, Oregon

NO BUSINESS AS USUAL
Sermons for the Lectionary, Year A, Pentecost through Christ the King

Copyright © 2019 Bruce L. Taylor. All rights reserved. Except for brief quotations in critical publications or reviews, no part of this book may be reproduced in any manner without prior written permission from the publisher. Write: Permissions, Wipf and Stock Publishers, 199 W. 8th Ave., Suite 3, Eugene, OR 97401.

Wipf & Stock
An Imprint of Wipf and Stock Publishers
199 W. 8th Ave., Suite 3
Eugene, OR 97401

www.wipfandstock.com

PAPERBACK ISBN: 978-1-5326-9480-6
HARDCOVER ISBN: 978-1-5326-9481-3
EBOOK ISBN: 978-1-5326-9482-0

Manufactured in the U.S.A.   OCTOBER 1, 2019

Scripture quotations are from Common Bible: New Revised Standard Version Bible, copyright © 1989 National Council of the Churches of Christ in the United States of America. Used by permission. All rights reserved worldwide. The italics are the author's.

Additional scripture quotations are from the Revised Standard Version of the Bible, copyright © 1946, 1952, and 1971 National Council of the Churches of Christ in the United States of America. Used by permission. All rights reserved worldwide. The italics are the author's.

Translation of "Anaweza bwana" is used by permission of the All Africa Council of Churches.

Excerpts from *The Parables of Jesus* by George A. Buttrick, Copyright 1928 by Harper & Brothers. Used by permission of Rachel Crumpler.

Excerpt from the script of *The African Queen* courtesy of Romulus Films Ltd.

In memory of James H. Smylie, Austin C. Lovelace,
Clarence B. Ammons, Joseph Hadley, and
Gláucia Vasconcelos Wilkey—mentors, models, friends.

Contents

Introduction   xiii

THE DAY OF PENTECOST
Spanish Springs Presbyterian Church, Sparks, Nevada—May 11, 2008
Acts 2:1–21; 1 Corinthians 12:3b–13; John 20:19–23
"The Mission of Love"   1

TRINITY SUNDAY
Spanish Springs Presbyterian Church, Sparks, Nevada—May 30, 1999
Genesis 1:1—2:4a; 2 Corinthians 13:11–13; Matthew 28:16–20
"The Creator's Delight"   6

NINTH SUNDAY IN ORDINARY TIME
Spanish Springs Presbyterian Church, Sparks, Nevada—June 2, 2002
Genesis 6:9–22; 7:24; 8:1, 14–19; Romans 1:16–17; 3:21–31; Matthew 7:21–29
"The Faith of God"   11

TENTH SUNDAY IN ORDINARY TIME
Spanish Springs Presbyterian Church, Sparks, Nevada—June 5, 2005
Genesis 12:1–9; Romans 4:13–25; Matthew 9:9–13, 18–26
"Reaching Out and Letting Go"   16

ELEVENTH SUNDAY IN ORDINARY TIME
Spanish Springs Presbyterian Church, Sparks, Nevada —June 13, 1999
Genesis 18:1–15; 21:1–7; Romans 5:1–8; Matthew 9:35—10:8
"Work in Progress"   21

TWELFTH SUNDAY IN ORDINARY TIME
Spanish Springs Presbyterian Church, Sparks, Nevada—June 22, 2008
Genesis 21:8–21; Romans 6:1b–11; Matthew 10:24–42
"God's Other Life"   27

Contents

THIRTEENTH SUNDAY IN ORDINARY TIME
Spanish Springs Presbyterian Church, Sparks, Nevada—June 26, 2005
Genesis 22:1–14; Romans 6:12–23; Matthew 10:40–42
"The Test"   33

FOURTEENTH SUNDAY IN ORDINARY TIME
Spanish Springs Presbyterian Church, Sparks, Nevada—July 6, 2008
Genesis 24:34–38, 42–49, 58–67; Romans 7:15–25a; Matthew 11:16–19, 25–30
"Will the Real Me Please Stand Up?"   41

FIFTEENTH SUNDAY IN ORDINARY TIME
First Presbyterian Church, Norfolk, Nebraska—July 15, 1990
Genesis 25:19–34; Romans 8:1–11; Matthew 13:1–9, 18–23
"The Promise in the Seed"   46

SIXTEENTH SUNDAY IN ORDINARY TIME
First Presbyterian Church, Dodge City, Kansas—July 18, 1993
Genesis 28:10–19a; Romans 8:12–25; Matthew 13:24–30, 36–43
"Promise to a Coyote"   51

SEVENTEENTH SUNDAY IN ORDINARY TIME
First Presbyterian Church, Ponca City, Oklahoma—July 27, 2014
Genesis 29:15–28; Romans 8:26–39; Matthew 13:31–33, 44–52
"Hidden Certainty"   56

EIGHTEENTH SUNDAY IN ORDINARY TIME
First Presbyterian Church, Ponca City, Oklahoma—August 3, 2014
Genesis 32:22-31; Romans 9:1–5; Matthew 14:13–21
"The Crippling Victory"   62

NINETEENTH SUNDAY IN ORDINARY TIME
First Presbyterian Church, Dodge City, Kansas—August 8, 1993
Genesis 37:1–4, 12–28; Romans 10:5–15; Matthew 14:22–33
"Why Fear the Wind?"   68

TWENTIETH SUNDAY IN ORDINARY TIME
First Presbyterian Church, Dodge City, Kansas—August 15, 1993
Genesis 45:1–15; Romans 11:1–2a, 29–32; Matthew 15:10–28
"God's Way with Evil"   73

Contents

TWENTY-FIRST SUNDAY IN ORDINARY TIME
Spanish Springs Presbyterian Church, Sparks, Nevada—August 24, 2008
Exodus 1:8—2:10; Romans 12:1–8; Matthew 16:13–20
"Human Fear and Divine Promise"   78

TWENTY-SECOND SUNDAY IN ORDINARY TIME
Spanish Springs Presbyterian Church, Sparks, Nevada—September 1, 2002
Exodus 3:1–15; Romans 12:9–21; Matthew 16:21–28
"Prescription for an Icy Heart"   83

TWENTY-THIRD SUNDAY IN ORDINARY TIME
Spanish Springs Presbyterian Church, Sparks, Nevada—September 4, 2005
Exodus 12:1–14; Romans 13:8–14; Matthew 18:15–20
"Not for Empire"   88

TWENTY-FOURTH SUNDAY IN ORDINARY TIME
Spanish Springs Presbyterian Church, Sparks, Nevada—September 11, 2011
Exodus 14:19–31; Romans 14:5–12; Matthew 18:21–35
"The Hardest Thing"   94

TWENTY-FIFTH SUNDAY IN ORDINARY TIME
Spanish Springs Presbyterian Church, Sparks, Nevada—September 21, 2008
Exodus 16:2–15; Philippians 1:21–30; Matthew 20:1–16
"Justice"   99

TWENTY-SIXTH SUNDAY IN ORDINARY TIME
Spanish Springs Presbyterian Church, Sparks, Nevada—September 26, 1999
Exodus 17:1–7; Philippians 2:1–13; Matthew 21:23–32
"The Way Christians Count"   104

TWENTY-SEVENTH SUNDAY IN ORDINARY TIME
Spanish Springs Presbyterian Church, Sparks, Nevada—October 5, 2008
Exodus 20:1–4, 7–9, 12–20; Philippians 3:4b–14; Matthew 21:33–46
"Grateful for Salvation"   109

TWENTY-EIGHTH SUNDAY IN ORDINARY TIME
Spanish Springs Presbyterian Church, Sparks, Nevada—October 13, 2002
Exodus 32:1–14; Philippians 4:1–9; Matthew 22:1–14
"No Business as Usual"   114

Contents

TWENTY-NINTH SUNDAY IN ORDINARY TIME
Spanish Springs Presbyterian Church, Sparks, Nevada—October 19, 2008
Exodus 33:12–23; 1 Thessalonians 1:1–10; Matthew 22:15–22
"The Glory of God"   119

THIRTIETH SUNDAY IN ORDINARY TIME
First Presbyterian Church, Ponca City, Oklahoma—October 26, 2014
Deuteronomy 34:1–12; 1 Thessalonians 2:1–8; Matthew 22:34–46
"Leadership and Followership"   127

THIRTY-FIRST SUNDAY IN ORDINARY TIME
Spanish Springs Presbyterian Church, Sparks, Nevada—October 30, 2005
Joshua 3:7–17; 1 Thessalonians 2:9–13; Matthew 23:1–12
"Muddy Feet"   132

ALL SAINTS' DAY
Spanish Springs Presbyterian Church, Sparks, Nevada—November 1, 2011
Revelation 7:9–17; 1 John 3:1–3; Matthew 5:1–12
"The Inheritance"   137

THIRTY-SECOND SUNDAY IN ORDINARY TIME
First Presbyterian Church, Dodge City, Kansas—November 10, 1996
Joshua 24:1–3a, 14–25; 1 Thessalonians 14:13–18; Matthew 25:1–13
"Prepared for the Best"   142

THIRTY-THIRD SUNDAY IN ORDINARY TIME
Spanish Springs Presbyterian Church, Sparks, Nevada—November 16, 2008
Judges 4:1–7; 1 Thessalonians 5:1–11; Matthew 25:14–30
"It's Not About Us"   147

CHRIST THE KING
Spanish Springs Presbyterian Church, Sparks, Nevada—November 21, 1999
Ezekiel 34:11–16, 20–24; Ephesians 1:15–23; Matthew 25:31–46
"Faces of the King"   152

THANKSGIVING
Spanish Springs Presbyterian Church, Sparks, Nevada—November 27, 2002
Deuteronomy 8:1–10; Philippians 4:6–20; Matthew 6:25–33
"The Good Thing About Hunger"   159

Contents

APPENDIX: "Praying Our Way to San Jose"
St. John's Presbyterian Church, Reno, Nevada—June 25, 2008
Micah 6:1–8; 1 Timothy 2:1–3; Matthew 7:21–29
"Theme for a Prophetic Church"   **165**

List of Sources Cited   171

Introduction

In the churches in which I grew up, as well as the one in which I served as a seminary intern, the Sundays between Epiphany and Ash Wednesday and between Pentecost and the first Sunday in Advent were ordered as following Epiphany and Pentecost, respectively. That is, for instance, the third Sunday following Epiphany was designated liturgically as "The Third Sunday after Epiphany." When the Presbyterian and many other Protestant denominations adopted the custom of identifying these periods of the Christian calendar as "Ordinary Time", it seemed that the term implied an assignment (or demotion?) of these Sundays to the status of "nothing special." In the 1990s, my education in liturgical theology became more intentional, largely through participating in the Pastor as Liturgical Theologian program of the Presbyterian Church (U.S.A.)'s Office of Theology and Worship. I came to learn that the word "ordinary" in this case derived from the word "order" or "ordered" or perhaps "ordinal," indicating the annual numbered sequence of Sundays that fall outside of Advent, Christmastide/Day of Epiphany, Lent, and Eastertide/Day of Pentecost.

Popular opinion and the church's own bustling attention to those other liturgical seasons still burdens the term "Ordinary Time" with a connotation of typicality that parallels the sense among both clergy and laity that Advent, Christmas, Lent, and Easter are "extra-ordinary." When they are over, "we can get back to normal," visually meaning week upon week of green paraments and green vestments, and tepid worship attendance.

The story of Easter, of course, declares that, in reality, there is no such thing as "ordinary" time for the Christian or even for an unbelieving world. Everything has changed. Everything has been made new. Every moment is pregnant with the possibility of God's ultimate and imminent fulfillment

Introduction

of the promise of completion and redemption. Every day calls for alert and responsive adherence to the teachings and example of Jesus, now the risen Christ. Indeed, the veil between life in the kingdom of the world and life in the kingdom of heaven has now been forever lifted for those who have eyes to see and hearts to accept. We may count ordinally the Sundays each year that we trustfully and expectantly await the return of Christ and the vanquishing of the world's powers and principalities, knowing that the number of the days until God's final act of redemption is staged grows ever shorter, but they all amount to but an instant in the mind of God. In the meantime, the resurrection faith transcends any season of the calendar and the Spirit works freely under, above, and beyond the church's penitential seasons and high feast days. Every Sunday, as Martin Luther observed, is a little Easter, even the ones in the middle of a frigid winter or a sultry summer, and so lethargy must not be our habit and cynicism has no place in our outlook.

Matthew's Gospel, which is featured in Year A of the Common Lectionary, addresses the outlook and behavior of followers of Jesus Christ that will characterize the vocation of faithful discipleship in every season. Many of the readings from Matthew during Ordinary Time about the education and experience of the twelve constitute instructions for the evangelist's own congregation, often in the face of criticism and harassment if not actual persecution. Sermons expounding these readings challenge and exhort contemporary followers of Christ to faithfulness in daily encounters within family, within the church, and in the culture to which Christ sends them to make more disciples in every neighborhood, baptizing in the name of the Father and of the Son and of the Holy Spirit and teaching obedience to everything that Jesus commanded his first disciples.

As I noted in a previous volume, *The Word in the Wind*, the sermon need not and, indeed, cannot bear the entire task of unfolding the layers of meaning in the day's lections. Thoughtful and intentional preparation of the liturgy is just as important as thoughtful and intentional preparation of the sermon. Music is an important component of liturgical worship, and the congregation's song is central to the work of the people. Fortunately, the growing use of the lectionary over the past few decades has inspired a flowering of hymnody that has answered the opportunity of providing worshipers with fresh words to sing in learning and responding to the testimony of scripture. Many newer hymns focus on biblical texts and themes that have been overlooked by previous generations of hymn writers, sometimes engaging modern believers more meaningfully in ancient events otherwise dusty and remote.

The Common Lectionary (Revised) offers us stories of the extraordinary love of God throughout the course of Ordinary Time, including the long

Introduction

stretch of Sundays from Pentecost to Christ the King, which is now often called the Reign of Christ. In *The Word in the Wind*, I offered a collection of sermons for Year A of the lectionary from the First Sunday of Advent through the Seventh Sunday of Easter. The present volume comprises a compilation of sermons for the second half of Year A in the lectionary cycle that contemplates the daily implications of what the annual festivals of Christmas and Easter herald, including a sampling of sermons in the form of stories. They show that, for the person whose faith has been awakened by the events celebrated on the high feast days, there can be no such thing as business as usual on any other day of the year. Also included are a sermon for the secular but theologically rich national holiday of Thanksgiving, for which the Common Lectionary provides readings, and, in an appendix, a sermon preached at the invitation of the Presbyterian Church (U.S.A.)'s committee which planned a series of worship events preceding the denomination's 218th General Assembly meeting in San Jose, California, in the summer of 2008. Many of the sermons reflect, either implicitly or by direct reference, the time and place in which they were originally delivered. I have elected to include them without revision for specific recent events. Most dramatically, perhaps, the premise of the sermon titled "Human Fear and Divine Promise" has become tragically even more poignant. In all cases, I believe, history has only added to, rather than subtracted from, their pertinence. I encourage the reading of the lections listed for each sermon prior to reading the sermon itself.

In one way or another, all of the sermons in this collection offer testimony to the truth that Ordinary Time is a fruitful season for proclaiming and celebrating the extraordinary work of God in the person of the living Lord Jesus Christ through the power of the Holy Spirit. May each of us rejoice constantly that God is never absent from the beloved creation, and that Christ is able to transform the mundane and the routine into the heaven-imbued and the exceptional, meaning that no circumstance is hopeless and no moment lies outside the divine timetable of salvation.

The Day of Pentecost

Spanish Springs Presbyterian Church, Sparks, Nevada

May 11, 2008

Acts 2:1–21
1 Corinthians 12:3b–13
John 20:19–23

"The Mission of Love"

For you and me, twenty centuries after the disciples "were all together in one place" (Acts 2:1b, NRSV), Pentecost is a date on a calendar, one that changes from year to year depending upon when Easter occurs. Indeed, when it happens to fall on the second Sunday of May, the religious holiday can seem quite secondary to the secular celebration of *Mother's Day*, even in some *churches*. But long before Mother's Day was invented, long before the affection that family members should have for one another was turned to profit, Pentecost was celebrated throughout the Christian community as the birthday of the church, dated from the bestowal of the Holy Spirit upon Christ's followers.

Can you imagine the excitement of that Pentecost long ago, when, after waiting for they-knew-not-exactly-what, something totally unprecedented happened to the disciples who were gathered together? There was "a sound like the rush of a violent wind," the book of Acts says, "and it filled the entire house where they were sitting. Divided tongues, as of fire, appeared among them, and a tongue rested on each of them. All of them were filled with the Holy Spirit and began to speak in other languages, as the Spirit gave them ability" (Acts 2:2–4, NRSV). But the experience was not to be a private affair,

The Day of Pentecost

and it was not for personal gratification, nor was it meant to create a spiritual elitism. "Now there were devout Jews from every nation under heaven living in Jerusalem. And at this sound the crowd gathered and was bewildered, because each one heard them speaking in the native language of each" (Acts 2:5–6, NRSV).

Here is a biblical story that Hollywood, to my knowledge, has never tackled. It's just as well; perhaps we, each of us, should be allowed to picture it in our own imagination. It might just be *too* spectacular for the silver screen, even in this age of computer-generated special effects. It's spectacular *enough* in the *telling*, and has sparked a lot of fantastic claims over the history of Christianity, not least of which is the whole matter of speaking in tongues. But it's not at all about the disciples suddenly speaking an unknown super-spiritual language of heaven. These were words that people in other parts of the world used in common, everyday speech. What Acts is saying is that people who had come to Jerusalem from every corner of the earth for the feast of Pentecost heard and understood what the disciples had to say.

> Amazed and astonished, they asked, "Are not all these who are speaking *Galileans*? And how is that we hear, each of us, in our own native language? Parthians, Medes, Elamites, and residents of Mesopotamia, Judea and Cappadocia, Pontus and Asia, Phrygia and Pamphylia, Egypt and the parts of Libya belonging to Cyrene, and visitors from Rome, both Jews and proselytes, Cretans and Arabs—in our own languages we hear them speaking about God's deeds of power." (Acts 2:7–11, NRSV; emphasis here and in subsequent scripture quotations has been added)

Luke, whom we believe was the author of Acts, was clearly impressed with the supernatural aspect of tongues as of fire and the disciples speaking suddenly in foreign languages, and that scene grabs *our* attention, *too*. But we shouldn't let our curiosity about the spectacular features of the story obscure the substance of what was going on: the disciples, only just recently fearful and disavowing any relationship to Jesus, timid and uncertain following the death of their Master, were now testifying to God's deeds of power, and people representing every nation on earth were listening and hearing. Peter, the very one who had denied even *knowing* Jesus on the night of his arrest, suddenly became bold and articulate, and the others soon followed his lead. And the rest of the book of Acts shows how the proclamation of God's deeds of power in Jesus Christ spread from Jerusalem through Judea and Syria and all the way to Rome.

But although this passage from Acts about the coming of the Holy Spirit is the story most of us think of, *Luke's* account of the coming of the Spirit upon

"The Mission of Love"

the disciples as Jesus had promised is not the *only* account of the coming of the Holy Spirit in the New Testament. What Luke interprets as having taken fifty days to happen after the resurrection, the Fourth Gospel interprets as having happened on the very night after Jesus' tomb was discovered to be empty.

> When it was evening on that day, the first day of the week, and the doors of the house where the disciples had met were locked for fear of the Jews, Jesus came and stood among them and said, "Peace be with you." After he said this, he showed them his hands and his side. Then the disciples rejoiced when they saw the Lord. Jesus said to them again, "Peace be with you. As the Father has sent me, so I send you." When he had said this, he breathed on them and said to them, "Receive the Holy Spirit. If you forgive the sins of any, they are forgiven them; if you retain the sins of any, they are retained." (John 20:19-23, NRSV)

Hollywood hasn't given us a movie version of *that* episode, *either*, maybe because the studios wouldn't know what to make of it—*John's* account of the gift of the Holy Spirit isn't flashy *enough*, despite the implication that Jesus was able to walk through a locked door, just as he had been raised from a sealed tomb. But we don't have to regard the different accounts as contradicting each other. It isn't a matter of accepting one story and rejecting the other. As it so often does, John's Gospel is more interpretive of events that Matthew, Mark, and Luke tell more journalistically. And it's not just an issue of *when* it occurred. Where *Luke*, in the book of Acts, says that the foreigners heard from the disciples in their own language about God's deeds of power, the first installment of the witness that the disciples were to make "in Jerusalem, in all Judea and Samaria, and to the ends of the earth" (Acts 1:8b, NRSV), *John* specifies that the Spirit-empowered mission of the disciples was the work of *forgiving and retaining sins*. And whereas, in *Luke*, the Spirit was something that Jesus had said he was going to send (and so it happens in Acts many days separate and apart from the presence of Christ, who has already ascended to heaven), in *John*, the granting of the Spirit is a personal delivery—as personal as Jesus' own breath, breathed out upon the disciples as they have just verified that the *resurrected Christ* standing *before* them is the *same* person as the *crucified Jesus* who was buried in the *tomb*. John leaves no doubt that it is Jesus' own Spirit that is being bestowed (the same word in Greek means both "spirit" and "breath"), and it is Jesus' own ministry that the disciples will be carrying on. And it is inextricably related to Christ's greeting and gift of peace.

The bestowal of the Holy Spirit, in John, is, as we noted, related to the forgiveness of sins: "If you *forgive* the sins of any, they are *forgiven* them; if you *retain* the sins of any, they are *retained*" (John 20:23, NRSV). The authority to forgive and retain sins is a power that troubles a good many Christians who are loathe to exercise what seems to be a very weighty responsibility; surely it should be up to *God* to forgive or not. The Roman Catholic Church points to this passage to support the practice of priests absolving people of their sins, and imposing conditions of penance in exchange for forgiveness. Protestants note that it was apparently to Jesus' followers in *general* that the authority was granted; John does not limit the number of people to whom Jesus said this to a mere *eleven*—the twelve minus Judas. But, John says, the work of forgiving or retaining sins is what Jesus was commissioning the disciples to do, and, in his proclaiming it to the church, John wants all Christians to know that *this* is the church's work whenever and wherever the church exists and is faithful. And what the church is doing when it *does* so is continuing the work of *Jesus*—"As *you* have sent *me* into the world," he prayed to the Father on the night before he was arrested, "so *I* have sent *them* into the world" (John 17:18, NRSV). The gift that Jesus bestows by breathing upon the disciples is the gift of the Spirit which empowers the community to continue the work of Jesus. As God's breath gave life to our first ancestor so long ago, Jesus' breathing upon his disciples gives the church *its* life. A new, second creation has come into being, and it is sustained not by its *own* initiative, not through its *own* ingenuity, but *only* and *always* as *Jesus*' doing. Jesus shares with his followers the life-force that dwelled in him and brought him forth from the grave.

What Jesus' *disciples* are to do is no different from what *he* did. And that is to speak and do the words and signs that cause people to believe, if they but choose to do so. At the *beginning* of the Gospel of John, we are told that John the Baptist's role was to testify to Jesus, so that all might believe through him. At the original *ending* of John, just a few verses after today's reading, John tells us that what he has written is so that people might come to believe that Jesus is the Messiah, the Son of God, and that through believing they may have life in his name. In John, sin is not specific acts of transgression, but blindness to the revelation of God in Christ—failure to see in Jesus the person and personality of God. Jesus' commission to the disciples, and their empowerment with the Holy Spirit, to forgive or retain sins, is the authority and assignment to *continue* what God sent *Jesus* to do. And *that* is the work of *love*. "For God so loved the world that he gave his only Son, so that everyone who believes in him may not perish but may have eternal life" (John 3:16, NRSV). The mission of each disciple and the whole church is to reveal God by showing God's love.

To reveal God's love the way that *Jesus* did is a daunting task. Just think of Jesus turning water into wine, of feeding five thousand with a few loaves of bread and even fewer fish, of crossing barriers of ethnicity and respectability and even religion, of giving sight to people long blind, of raising the dead back

"The Mission of Love"

to life again. As we read of Jesus' activities in John, each successively reveals more profoundly God's power, and each successively deals more assertively with sin as John understands it—blindness to who Jesus is, the Son of God fully endowed with the Holy Spirit. "Very truly, I tell you," Jesus had said to his disciples the night before his crucifixion, "the one who believes in me will also do the works that I do and, in fact, will do greater works than these, because I am going to the Father" (John 14:12, NRSV). It was as he was going to the Father that Jesus breathed the Holy Spirit upon the church to continue his work on an even broader scale. Who was still unforgiven? Who was still joyless? Who was still hungry? Who was still discriminated against and outcast? Who still could not see? Who was still bound and shut up in a tomb? The mission Jesus was giving his disciples—not just the few huddled in a house fearful and uncertain on the evening of the day Jesus' burial place was discovered to be empty, but *all* of us—was to love the world into joy, to love the world into fullness of stomach, to love the world into community, to love the world into clear vision, to love the world into eternal life—to reveal God. An impossible task, you say? Not when the church is breathing in the Holy Spirit—the Spirit which is given us not to tear down, but to build up, not to separate us, but to unite us, not to condemn, but to save—the Spirit that enables us to show the whole world that God is love!

In the 1960s, a popular television show began each week's episode with the words, "Your mission, Mr. Phelps, should you choose to accept it . . ." The mission of the disciples of Jesus Christ, week after week, day after day, is always the same—to cure blindness by giving witness to the light that reveals God in the continuing ministry of Jesus Christ and thus to raise people to eternal life. Not just attending worship, important as that is. Not just being a congregation member, significant as that is. Not just giving financially, necessary as that is. But being fully and always engaged in the mission of love. "As the Father has sent me," Jesus said, "so I send you" (John 20:21b, NRSV). Peace be with you.

Trinity Sunday

Spanish Springs Presbyterian Church, Sparks, Nevada

May 30, 1999

Genesis 1:1—2:4a
2 Corinthians 13:11–13
Matthew 28:16–20

"The Creator's Delight"

Imagine that *you* had been there when the unthinkable had happened—pagan soldiers from a foreign land had invaded the little place that God had given to your ancestors long ago with a promise that it would *always* be yours. Your fields had been devastated. Your capital city had been laid waste. The best and brightest of your fellow citizens had been carried off to a distant exile, perhaps *you* along *with* them, refugees in a program not so much of "ethnic cleansing" but national dismemberment. Finally, you hear news even more horribly incredible than the conquest itself: the temple of God built by King Solomon centuries ago has been reduced to rubble, looted and burned and toppled stone from stone.

    The triumphant nation that has dismantled your worldview and ridiculed your hopes worships a whole encyclopedia of gods, and undoubtedly they are loudly attributing their military success to the power of their idols. And in time, as you sit bewildered in a strange land far from home and watch the workings of this other society, its continued successes in brutal battle and the lavish treasures that its generals bring home and parade arrogantly through the streets, you begin to wonder, is there maybe some truth to the claims they

"The Creator's Delight"

make about their gods? Are the names they worship indeed more powerful than the God of Abraham and Sarah, Isaac and Rebekah, Jacob and Rachel? They tell you that their gods shine in the sky, some of them—the sun by day and the moon and the stars by night. Mortals are subject to their whims, they say, for they are not emotionally involved with humankind or much interested in what happens to them; men and women are but meaningless pawns on some divine chessboard. The best that human beings can hope for is to appease their silly fancies. What happens to us and to the world around us is not even guided by fate, really, but by divine caprice, softened perhaps by the expectation of amusement or profit. And, over time, it begins to sound plausible, for why *else* would a Babylon be victor over an Israel?

Some such questions must come to the minds of *any* people who feel defeated—defeated by an army, defeated by an illness, defeated by poverty, or defeated by slander. Of course, the prophets had warned the Israelites that their unfaithfulness would have consequences, but the expediencies of the moment always seemed so much more important—or at least so much more rewarding—than proper attention to worship, to justice, and to the poor. They had been taught from infancy that they were *God's* people, after all, and didn't that surely mean that no idol-worshipers could ever really threaten them, much less defeat them? And even if a *righteous* God might permit the *people* to be punished for their disobedience, why would a *powerful* God ever allow the humiliating destruction of the *temple*?

Fortunately, by the power of the Spirit, faith stirred in some of the exiles from Israel as they were held captive in Babylon. They recalled that God had promised never to abandon them. They reaffirmed that no human army could defeat God's purpose of redeeming creation. They reasserted that the claims the Babylonians made for *their* gods were absurd. And they began to give new voice to their faith. They retold the ancient stories. They remembered the ancient truths. They sang of their trust in the one true God whose promise is steadfast and whose care is dependable in spite of every temporary evidence God's enemies could claim.

"In the beginning when *God* created the heavens and the earth" (Gen 1:1a, NRSV); and *God* said . . . And *God* made . . . And *God* saw that it was good . . . Did someone say that the sun and moon and stars were *gods*? Pooh! The God of Israel's ancestors made them—the stars that shine over Babylon as well as the stars that shine over Israel! Did someone say that animals and trees exist just for pleasure and exploitation? Pooh! God made them, too, each one a handiwork of God and therefore a treasure, not for mindless waste but as an integral part of God's creative purpose. Did someone say that humankind exists as merely the playthings of the gods, or that one race is superior or that

Trinity Sunday

one nation is supreme or that one sex is more important? Pooh! God created humankind without passports and without flags, and both men and women are equally the image of God, which means that God must be just as *feminine* as God is *masculine*. Did someone say that one day is just like the next, an endless repetition of what has been, without meaning and without destiny? Pooh! As part and parcel of the creation itself, "on the seventh day God finished the work that he had done, and he rested on the seventh day from all the work that he had done. So God blessed the seventh day and hallowed it, because on it God rested from all the work that he had done in creation" (Gen 2:2–3 NRSV). And on every *eighth* day, God *continues* to move purposefully toward the *perfection* of the creation, in partnership with what God has already made.

And so Israel declared its faith that the god *it* worshiped is the God who created everything that is, the God who is sovereign over everything that is, the God who will bend everything and redeem every situation so that it fulfills the loving purpose God had from the very moment of deciding that it was not good for *God* to be alone. God will not let the chosen people wither away. God will not let destruction and dismay be the last words. God will do whatever is necessary, and God *can* do whatever is necessary—the same God who delighted to put the stars in the sky and the water in the ocean and the grass in the field will not let chaos again take over the universe or even your world or mine.

Any army, any party, any class that thinks the world is its oyster to pry open and snatch the pearl while God looks the other way either does not understand or does not care that God is the Creator, made everything that is for the purpose of loving communion, and wants every creature to have its own share of the fruits and potentialities of creation. When the people of Israel forgot that—when they began to take pride in their own accomplishments, their own technologies and their own schemes; when they began to exploit the poor and abuse the powerless; when they began to trust in their military might and their economy; when they began to neglect worship and turn their sabbath into a day for profit—then the collapse of their nation was assured. Drawing on the limited science of the times and the character that God had always shown, and remembering the promise, the writer of Genesis put Israel's faith in context. He reminded the people dejected and bewildered in exile that the God who loved Israel into being was the God who loved the whole *world* into being for a purpose that no army could defeat and no sin could spoil. All of creation and each person in it is the Creator's own delight. How could King Nebuchadnezzar and all his Babylonian idols match the Truth that made the universe with a word? How could any army, how could any illness, how could any deed of injustice or instance of oppression, how could any cruel word or

"The Creator's Delight"

act by any human being defeat someone who knows that he or she has been wonderfully loved into existence by the same God who made the earth and the heavens?

We don't know exactly when Matthew's Gospel was written, except that it was probably a few years after Jerusalem had *again* been destroyed by a foreign army from a pagan land—this time, Rome—and the temple that *King Herod* had built had been toppled. Again, the unthinkable had happened. Again, there must have been faith-testing and gut-wrenching questions about where the God of Israel was when it was all happening, whether this God had lost power even to save the great house of holy worship. Some people might have remembered wondering, many years earlier as they watched Jesus die on the cross, where God was *that* day, that dark and gruesome Friday, and whether this God had lost power even to save his Son.

The evangelist was writing his Gospel for people in exile—Christians of Jewish background living in Syria after the Roman destruction of Jerusalem. In *his* faith community, there was probably a fair amount of bewilderment and uncertainty about God's seeming powerlessness to stop the pagan rampage. But the evangelist reminded his Christian readers that what had appeared to be *powerlessness* on *Good Friday* laid the necessary foundation for God's mightiest act of *redemption* on *Easter Sunday*—the redemption of his own Son from the grip of death. The creative power that by a word brought forth life on the face of the earth with all its variety and all its complexity and all its amazing interdependence, had also brought forth life from the grave. The God who made a precious promise to the people Israel long ago now, in Christ himself, made a *new* promise *just* as precious: "And remember, I am with you always, to the end of the age" (Matt 28:20b, NRSV). Creation was still the Creator's delight. The people would still not be abandoned, though nations and even temples might fall.

And the comprehensive breadth of the promise became newly apparent in the words of the risen Christ himself to his followers: "Go therefore and make disciples of *all* nations, baptizing them in the name of the Father and of the Son and of the Holy Spirit, and teaching them to obey everything that I have commanded you" (Matt 28:19-20a, NRSV)—they were to make known throughout the world the commandments about love of God and love of neighbor and who God is and who our *neighbor* is, the commandments about trust and dependability, the commandments about witness and devotion, the commandments about forgiveness and self-sacrifice. And all of that was for the Creator's loving purpose of restoring creation to the fullness that the Creator intended, the Creator's absolute delight. God's creation is not a place where humankind and other creatures exist to be abused by a cruel and capricious tyrant, but a place where the Creator freely shares creative power and responsibility. God's creation is not a place where the Creator might shut us away when we bore or tire or exasperate the one who made us, but a place where every conceivable measure has been taken for our permanent joy and well-being. God's creation is a place where there is sufficient for all, if it is shared and not hoarded. God's creation is a place where no one and no thing feeds to the detriment of another, if pride and greed yield to forgiveness and generosity. God's creation is a place where every creature, animate and inanimate, is dear to God, rather than a place to be exploited and despoiled ruthlessly and without thought to future generations of all living things. God's creation is a place where the rhythms of creation itself are received as a gift of God, rather than something to be schemed around. God's creation is a place where truth is spoken in respect and love, rather than allowing fear and falsehood to work their destructive disharmony. Far from allowing them to feel defeated, and that creation was out of control and that life was without purpose, the risen Christ gave his followers a new commission in God's ongoing task of bringing creation to perfect fullness. On God's very own authority, Jesus declared that God *still* loves this creation, and all of his disciples are to testify to that boldly and continually in our words and in our actions toward all people everywhere. Creation is not God's whim. It is, and it will remain, God's delight.

Ninth Sunday in Ordinary Time
Spanish Springs Presbyterian Church, Sparks, Nevada
June 2, 2002

Genesis 6:9–22; 7:24; 8:1, 14–19
Romans 1:16–17; 3:21–31
Matthew 7:21–29

"The Faith of God"

Of all the stories in the Bible, I suppose that none is more well-known than the story of Noah and the flood. Certainly, no other biblical story has so captured the popular imagination and been turned into product lines from children's bedding to Bill Cosby records. But as often happens when a Bible story becomes public currency, details get lost, plot becomes simplified, and, in the process, the reason that the story is even *in* the Bible becomes obscured and its message becomes garbled. It becomes "de-biblified," if you will. So the vast majority of people who "know all about" Noah and the flood could not even tell you where to find it in the Bible. Like another story about salvation and perilous waters—the story of Jonah, the theological point of which is forgotten almost entirely in the popular fascination with the "great fish"—the fundamental truths of the Noah story usually get lost amidst cuddly pairs of stuffed animals in the gift shop. Driving to and from Wichita on presbytery business, I used to pass a church in the little town of Maize, Kansas, called "The Ark," built in the shape of a big boat—a statement that here was a place of safety and salvation. But driving through the St. Louis area en route to and from Virginia, where I was working on my PhD, I used to pass a hotel in St. Charles, Missouri, called "The Ark," and the animal theme (Noah wasn't depicted anywhere on the premises) showed that the whole motif was purely for the sake of novelty.

Almost anyone could tell you that the waters rose for forty days; very few people could tell you that the reason the Bible gives for the waters beginning to *subside* was that "God remembered Noah and all the wild animals and all the domestic animals that were with him in the ark" (Gen 8:1a, NRSV). Some will know that the story has something to do with a rainbow. Not many will be able to tell you that the bow in the clouds is a sign to remind *God* of the promise God gave to Noah that the waters shall never again become a flood to destroy all flesh.

And it wasn't just a matter of a lot of rain. The Bible says that, on the day it all began, "the fountains of the great deep burst forth, and the windows of the heavens were opened" (Gen 7:11b, NRSV). The chaos that God had tamed back in the beginning of the world, when God created a dome to separate the watery chaos and allow dry land to appear, had been unleashed again, waters gushing up from below the earth *as well as* raining down from the *sky*. It was as if God was giving up on creation entirely because of human wickedness, human disdain for the will of God and human disregard for the providence of God. It had all gone so sour, what God had intended as a delight and had seen and pronounced as good. It's no sacrilege to suggest that God's pride was bruised, just as a little bit of pride probably sneaks into all parents' decisions to mete out punishment upon disobedient children. But God's judgment here involved not just a suspension of television privileges; it involved utter annihilation. Did humankind think it could get along *without* God? Then just let everything be as it was before God entered the picture—a formless void, dark and lifeless!

As the story goes, the flood that God unleashed had just about *done* that, when "God remembered Noah and all the wild animals and all the domestic animals that were with him in the ark. And God made a wind blow over the earth, and the waters subsided" (Gen 8:1, NRSV). God remembered the little delegation of living creatures adrift on the angry sea, and God remembered that Noah, at least, had been righteous—not perfect, not without faults, but a person of integrity, who acknowledged the God-ness of God. And all God's disgust turned to pity. And all God's hurt turned to compassion. And all God's disappointment once again turned to hope. And God resolved to save creation. God caused all the churning, lethal waters to drain away back into their caverns under the earth, and the great boat that carried the seeds of life came to rest on a high mountain, and God called Noah and his family and the animals with them out of the ark and onto dry land, with the expressed intention that they would be fruitful and multiply.

"The Faith of God"

What had changed? Was there any prospect that human beings would be more pious *after* the flood than they had been *before* the flood? The future generations weren't even born yet; *they* wouldn't have learned any lesson. The Bible doesn't say anywhere that the people who came *after* Noah were better than the people of Noah's *own* generation. And the Bible doesn't say anywhere that God *expected* them to be. Indeed, God hadn't even yet seen what they were capable and *in*capable of when God told Noah, "I establish my covenant with you, that never again shall all flesh be cut off by the waters of a flood, and never again shall there be a flood to destroy the earth" (Gen 9:11, NRSV).

For Noah's part, the only thing necessary to keeping the covenant that God memorialized with the bow in the clouds was to be fruitful and multiply. Of course, producing a next generation is itself a sort of act of faith and hope in the continued goodness of creation—to keep on *being* the creation, the creation that God loves so profoundly that, ultimately, when push came to shove, so to speak, God found himself unable to allow it to be blotted out forever. Perhaps the reason is that, as told in the Bible, though God had every justification to have done with humankind by whatever means God chose, the flood story has less to do with God's anger and fury than with God's sorrow and pain, less to do with God's dignity and majesty than with God's disappointment and regret, less to do with God's rage and judgment than with God's love and mercy. No pop-up children's book of giraffes and hippos can do justice to the profound angst at work in the heart of God. Nor can a blithe assertion that God will bring an end to everything when things get wicked enough. The Noah story shows that God is personally and even emotionally caught up in the creation. And the Noah story shows that God has chosen, come what may, to stand *by* creation, to stand *with* creation, to stand *for* creation, eternally hopeful that it will fulfill God's loving intention, that it will live up to its potential of genuine fellowship, creature with creature, and creature with Creator. God, in other words, has faith in God's *purpose*.

The question of why Noah, of all the people on earth, was saved—he and his family—is answered in the first verse of our Old Testament reading today: "Noah was a righteous man, blameless in his generation; Noah walked with God" (Gen 6:9b–c, NRSV). One commentator has written that it took a great act of faith to begin building such a tremendously large boat while there was nary a cloud in the sky. But what prompted Noah's venture into ship-building was not a reading of the weather. It was an understanding of God, and God's purpose. And that understanding, that reading of the religious climate, was something that anybody with a sensitivity toward God and God's desires could and should have had. But only Noah was not so preoccupied with feasting and celebrating human achievements and milestones that he could sense

Ninth Sunday in Ordinary Time

the anguish in God's heart and hear the thunder rumbling beyond the horizon of human cares and human satisfactions. He was a righteous man, the Bible says. He walked with God. And he built an ark, based on his *faith in* God.

I find it interesting that Paul, in his letter to the Romans, explains the death of Jesus by saying that it was God's way of showing *his* righteousness: "it was to prove at the present time that *he himself* is righteous and that he justifies the one who has faith in Jesus" (Rom 3:26, NRSV). Now, the word "righteousness" in the Bible means acknowledging and faithfully performing those duties upon which a relationship with another person is based. When spoken of in terms of one's relationship to *God*, the concept of "righteousness" is intimately entwined with the notion of *faith*. Noah was "righteous." Noah did the things that showed he was in a proper relationship with God. Ultimately, Noah built an ark in the trusting faith that God willed to *save* Noah and his family and two of every kind of animal from destruction in the flood that was to come, though the sun was shining brightly. But what does it mean to say that *God* is "righteous"—in Paul's words, that God showed righteousness by putting forward Christ Jesus as a sacrifice of atonement? With whom does *God* need to be in a *proper* relationship? (After all, God is *God*!) What does it mean to suggest that God's *righteousness*—God's panoply of deeds honoring the duties of that relationship—is an expression of God's *faith*?

Whatever we may mean by the "omniscience of God," Genesis clearly shows that it cannot mean that God knew before entering into the adventure of creation that the earth would be corrupt and filled with violence; the fact that it *was*, in Noah's time, grieved and saddened God. It was a *surprise*, as well as a *sorrow*. But when God remembered Noah and all the animals that were with him in the ark, what God was remembering was the hope that had prompted God to create the world and animals and human beings in the first place—a hope for companionship in eternity—and commitment to what God created—to love it, to cherish it, to care for it, to provide for it, come what may, even as a mother and father care for their child. God's righteousness has to do with *God's own faith* in *God's own purpose*, and God's own faith that you and I are worth saving from the consequences of our faithless and *un*righteous *disregard* of God's purpose when we disobey the limits God has set and when we refuse to perform the duties God has commanded—the rather predictable consequences of trying to be our own God (which is idolatry). And in a great supreme act of righteous faith in God's purpose of a loving relationship through all eternity, God sacrificed Jesus his Son on the cross as proof to all—perhaps even proof to God *himself*—of God's unshakable commitment to the creation—rocks, trees, fish, reptiles, birds, and you and me.

"The Faith of God"

Salvation, Paul declares earlier in Romans, is not, then, a matter of *our* righteousness. We have in so many ways failed to honor *our* part of the relationship. Even our *worship* is imperfect, infected with our own interests, burdened with our concern of what is aesthetically pleasing to *us*. We turn the law, that God gave as a guide to perfect fellowship with God and with one another, into a drudgery and something by which we rationalize our own judgments upon one another, and an excuse for boasting of ourselves and condemning others. "But now, *apart* from the law, the righteousness of God has been disclosed, and is *attested* by the law and the prophets, the righteousness of God through faith in Jesus Christ for all who believe" (Rom 3:21–22a, NRSV)—for all who believe that God looks at the bow in the clouds and remembers his love for us, for all who believe that God looks upon our sin and sees the precious dearness that prompted him to give his own Son as an atoning sacrifice for our salvation.

> But God remembered Noah and all the wild animals and all the domestic animals that were with him in the ark. And God made a wind blow over the earth, and the waters subsided . . . Then God said to Noah, "Go out of the ark, you and your wife, and your sons and your sons' wives with you. Bring out with you every living thing that is with you of all flesh—birds and animals and every creeping thing that creeps on the earth—so that they may abound on the earth, and be fruitful and multiply on the earth." (Gen 8:1, 15–17, NRSV)

"The one who is righteous will live by faith" (Rom 1:17b, NRSV). "[T]here is no distinction, since all have sinned and fall short of the glory of God; they are now justified by his grace as a gift, through the redemption that is in Christ Jesus, whom God put forward as a sacrifice of atonement by his blood, effective through faith. He did this to show his righteousness" (Rom 3:22b–25a, NRSV). Christ's crucifixion and resurrection are the supreme proof of the faith of God.

Tenth Sunday in Ordinary Time
Spanish Springs Presbyterian Church, Sparks, Nevada
June 5, 2005

Genesis 12:1–9
Romans 4:13–25
Matthew 9:9–13, 18–26

"Reaching Out and Letting Go"

With just the sparest of descriptions, the book of Genesis reports the most momentous decision that any human being has ever made: "So Abram went, as the Lord had told him" (Gen 12:4a, NRSV). What preceded that is almost as brief: "Now the Lord said to Abram, 'Go from your country and your kindred and your father's house to the land that I will show you. I will make of you a great nation, and I will bless you, and make your name great, so that *you* will be a blessing. I will bless those who bless you, and the one who curses you *I* will curse; and in *you* all the families of the earth shall be blessed'" (Gen 12:1–3 NRSV). The same God who, Genesis testifies, was once so frustrated with humankind that he sent a flood to blot out the earth, now determined to make a covenant with Abram and his family forever, to bless them and make them a great people, and, *through* them, to bless every family on earth. And to that huge promise that gives shape and direction to all of history, that gives purpose and meaning to life, Genesis reports Abram's response as simply this: "So Abram went, as the Lord had told him" (Gen 12:4a, NRSV). And, almost as a footnote, we are informed that Abram took his brother's son, Lot, with him, and Sarai his wife, and their possessions and household, and set forth

"Reaching Out and Letting Go"

and went to Canaan. "Abram was seventy-five years old when he departed" (Gen 12:4b, NRSV).

The rest of the Bible—all the many chapters in the many books—is an elaboration, and explanation, of the working out of the promise that God made to Abram. And, as today's reading from Romans shows, the apostles of Christ perceived that the life, death, and resurrection of Jesus were the fulfilling of the covenant God made with Abram so many centuries before, the covenant that Abram embraced with his simple yet crucial response: "So Abram went, as the LORD had told him" (Gen 12:4a, NRSV).

In ancient Near Eastern culture, it was unheard of for someone to strike out to find their own future off and away from the family, for anyone to journey into a foreign land far beyond the horizon from the farm where he had been born and had grown up. Contrary to our American pioneer heritage, such individualism, being cut off from one's roots, was not considered a virtue, never recognized as a goal. And even if a *younger* person might chance it, might break with every tradition and go off on his own, someone as old as *Abram* was—seventy-five—would hardly set out to start life over at *his* age. But God had spoken, we know not how, and Abram had recognized God's voice, we know not how, and Abram had trusted God enough not to raise practical objections or even ask questions at all, apparently, and to commit not only his *own* future, but the future of his entire family and household, to the venture of pioneering in a place where, for all he knew, there might already be inhabitants who would not welcome his incursion or obligingly step aside. The way might be treacherous; certainly, the journey would be difficult. And where was it that he was going, anyway? Had he ever even heard of it before? He would not have seen travel brochures. He couldn't pick up a map at AAA. All he had to go on was the word of God.

In Abram's case, though, one place might have been as good as another. Where he was, where he had been all his life, held little prospect beyond the predictable sameness of one day after another. The great word of God's *promise* in Genesis comes only a few verses after the great word of *despair* in Genesis: "Now Sarai was barren; she had no child" (Gen 11:30, NRSV). In ancient culture, that little phrase was almost a death sentence. In fact, it *was* a death sentence, in a way; the *family* was *everything*, and if the family were to come to an end, if a man were to have no heirs to carry on the name and work the fields or tend the flocks, then his life was judged to be perhaps not a failure, but essentially pointless. Cruel and insensitive as it sounds, a marriage was thought to be unsuccessful if it produced no children. And without heirs, there was no need to have land. But that is just the reason that God's promise to Abram was so remarkable: God was pointing Abram toward a land, a broad land, which presumes a *need* for the land, room to grow and expand, and God was announcing that this old man—"already as good as dead" (Rom 4:19b, NRSV), as Paul indelicately put it—and this childless woman, his wife Sarai, would be the parents of a great nation, blessed by God and a blessing to the rest of the world.

Most people *these* days would want a good deal more to go on than *Abram* had. Before leaving the only home they had ever known, where life was comfortable if not outstanding, where they knew the source of their next meal and knew the people who would come to their aid if the crop failed or the sheep died or the well went dry, most people *today* would want some *guarantee* of their future. More than a travel brochure and a map, we would probably insist that it all be in writing, spelling out exactly what God was promising to do and where and when God was promising to do it, and we might check with our insurance agent to see if a policy could be issued to cover our actual expenses plus emotional damage if things didn't turn out just as expected. Abram not only didn't have those things; the very point of his faithfulness, and the very point of Paul's *writing* about Abram's faithfulness, is just that he *didn't* seek assurances or guarantees; the only assurance or guarantee that Abram required was the promise of God. His faithfulness is defined by the fact that as soon as God had spoken, Abram *did* as God *directed*. And the result, after episodes that flirted with doubt and temptations to take things into one's own hands, was the nation of Israel, a people whom God took specially to himself and fashioned to become a witness to all peoples about who God is and what God intends, and with whom you and I are put on a par through the faithfulness of Jesus Christ on the cross.

If the writer of Genesis had *ended* the story after Abram had set out from home with Lot his brother's son and his wife Sarai and the animals and servants, you and I would be *un*likely to vote for Abram as the "Most Likely to Succeed." He hadn't planned adequately before forging ahead. He hadn't asked the right questions, hadn't done enough research, hadn't hedged his bets. I have yet to find a church session that would consider doing anything like what Abram did, for instance. He might be a patriarch, we might applaud his faith, but, when it comes right down to it, we would judge him really to be rather rash and irresponsible. (Honestly, now, would you hold up Abram's quick decision to pack up and go as an example for your son or daughter, or for yourself?) Our Presbyterian way would not just be to demand a brochure and a map. We would appoint a committee to study the matter and make a recommendation before changing the status quo in any way. And if *money* were concerned . . .

"Reaching Out and Letting Go"

But the blessedness of Abram here lies not in his being cautious or organized or ambitious. The blessedness of Abram, and perhaps the blessedness of *any* human being, lies in acknowledging one's right relationship with God, trusting the sufficiency of God's provision for whatever life may bring us, and committing oneself to being a blessing for others. Faith is not about *speculation*, but about *action*. Saying that he believed in God but not doing what God *said* to do would not only have meant that Abram's faith was *false*, but also that Abram would have remained *childless*, unresponsive to the future God had planned for him and for Sarai and for their family that would never *be* if they were to remain safe and secure though unfruitful in Haran. And the rest of the world would have remained unblessed. The past was a bleak story; if there was to be a different future, Abram had to risk embracing the promise that God was holding out to him. And so, in the blink of an eye, without any calculating or scheming, Abram reached out to God, let go of the past, and threw himself into the future that was unknown to anyone but God. Abram could not foresee the end of his adventure, but he had the courage to begin. And *God* faithfully took care of the *rest*. And what the world *then*, and the world *now*, would call "reckless" and "irresponsible," God blessed as "faith."

The Bible doesn't tell us what God would have done if Abram had refused, had sat down and shaken his head and concluded that such an adventure was just too fraught with uncertainties. It seems to me that Abram was not the *only* one taking a risk here. *God* was taking a risk, *too*—the risk of being turned down, but also the risk that his offer would be accepted—and then that God would be bound in covenant to this man and his generations of progeny that weren't even born yet. Would they be worthy? Would they uphold their end of the bargain?

But God *took* the risk, and the Bible testifies that, for *his* part, God remained faithful all along, despite all of the missteps of the Israelites, including a few missteps by Abram himself. And finally, it was one of Abraham's own descendants, as Matthew shows Jesus to have been, that Paul testifies *fulfilled* God's original intention in seeking out Abram and making the covenant after the disappointing start to creation that ended with the flood: the redemption of the creation God loves through the faithfulness of Jesus, God's own Son but *also* reckoned a child of *Abraham*, and Jesus' death on the cross and resurrection from the tomb. And for anyone to confess Jesus Christ as Lord, and that God raised him from the dead, means to share the faith of Abraham whose covenant with God is fulfilled in Christ—to reach out from the shadows of stagnation and despair and let go of the safe and the familiar. Genealogy is no longer important, adhering to the Torah is no longer necessary, for the distinction between Abraham's biological family—the Jews—and Abraham's family by faith—Gentiles who have responded to *Christ* in faith—*that* distinction is forever overcome and set aside. The same God who gave life where there *was* none—the birds and the fish and the cattle and every creeping thing and man and woman—is the God who again gave life where there was none—a child to barren and childless Abraham and Sarah in their old age—and is the God who once again gave life where there *was* none—to the dead and buried Jesus—and is the God who yet again gives life where there was none—the quickening faith that leads people out from caverns of hopelessness into the full daylight of God's purpose of salvation. And this same God blesses and *continues* to bless *all* families of the earth through the faithful witness, by words and deeds, of people who are open to hearing God's call and are willing to act on it immediately, without question, without calculation, without regret.

"As Jesus was walking along, he saw a man called Matthew sitting at the tax booth; and he said to him, 'Follow me.' And he got up and followed him" (Matt 9:9, NRSV). That is a characteristic of disciples, according to Matthew—a willingness, without deliberation or debate, to trust Jesus—God's Son—enough to reach out from the ordinary expectations of life, the ordinary securities of life, the ordinary disappointments of life—and let go the past so that we can be part of God's future, to allow ourselves to be blessed by God and, by risking in faith, be a blessing to *others*. What if Abram had said "no," or even said he'd have to *think* about it? What if Matthew or any of the others of the twelve had said "no," or even said they'd have to *think* about it? Perhaps we begin to understand the *consequences* to God's passionate purpose of redeeming the world if *we* should say "no," or even "I'll have to think about it." The call of Christ may come at any moment to risk acting on faith so that *we* may be blessed *and* be a *blessing*. Faith in Jesus Christ means being ready, at *every* moment, to reach out and let go.

Eleventh Sunday in Ordinary Time

Spanish Springs Presbyterian Church, Sparks, Nevada

June 13, 1999

Genesis 18:1–15; 21:1–7
Romans 5:1–8
Matthew 9:35—10:8

"Work in Progress"

"Therefore," begins the fifth chapter of Paul's letter to the Romans, "since we are justified by faith" (Rom 5:1a, NRSV). *"Justified"*? If you are new to the Christian faith, or if you are just beginning to explore what it is all about, you may sometimes feel that, when you open the Bible, you find yourself in a whole new world of ideas and terms. In fact, it can be so intimidating that you just close the book and think that you'll try it again later. Oh, the stories in Genesis are pleasant enough, and intriguing. And the parables of Jesus ring with a truth that preachers' sermons often only manage to get in the way of. But a lot of the Old Testament you find frankly redundant and rather boring—believe me, hardly *anyone* gets excited by Leviticus,—and much of the Old Testament may seem far removed from where you live and the questions that you ask, and it is not sacrilegious to admit that quite a few of the New Testament epistles are rather tedious and technical. Take, for instance, this business about being "justified." That seems to be the very sort of religious jargon that would turn off people who are wondering whether or not Christianity is for *them*.

The word "justify" literally means to make right, to make correct, to make blameless, to make acceptable in the sight of another person. It is a term

Eleventh Sunday in Ordinary Time

borrowed from the legal world, and of course, any word that is at home someplace as earthy as a courtroom is going to have its limitations in explaining something that has to do with the spirit. The apostle Paul, who wrote the letter to the Christians at Rome, most of whom were of pagan background, was trying to answer for his readers their question of whether, since the death and resurrection of Christ, God still had any interest in the Jews. The Jews had believed that "justification"—that is, being made right in the sight of God—had to do with keeping the *law*—all of the rules and regulations that God had given to Moses and Moses had passed on to his people long ago, including things like circumcision and the sorts of food a righteous person could and could not eat. Was God still interested in the Jews after so many of them had rejected his own Son? Were the law and the prophets still important after Jesus had died on the cross and been raised from the tomb? And, so, was it important to continue to follow all of the Jewish laws?

Paul's answer, in a nutshell, is that the law is still important—it is, after all, a gift from God—but it is not the *keeping* of the law that makes us *right* with God. It is not the *law* that justifies us in God's sight. It is not our obeying the *law* that saves us, whether it be avoiding particular foods or keeping the Ten Commandments. Rather, we are justified by *faith*. We are made right, we are made correct, we are made blameless, we are made acceptable in God's sight, by the sheer grace of God when we have faith in Jesus Christ, God's own Son—when we believe that everything he did and said is the very truth of God, and when we trust in his promises and even stake our lives on them. Jesus, Paul testifies, was handed over to death for our sins, because of our sins, to pay the price for our sins, and Jesus was raised for justification, to demonstrate that God has forgiven us, to guarantee our salvation.

"Therefore, *since we are justified,*" writes Paul—justified by *faith*—"we have peace with God through our Lord Jesus Christ" (Rom 5:1, NRSV). And Paul goes on to talk about what peace with God means and what it implies and what it makes possible in our lives. The apostle explained that people who have faith in Jesus Christ have *already* been justified, have *already* been set right before God, have *already* been deemed correct by God, have *already* been reckoned blameless in God's judgment, have *already* become acceptable in God's sight. Paul was able to turn to the *difference* that that makes in people's lives. We can get on with living out the life of people who have had God's love poured into their hearts through the Holy Spirit that has been given to them. Do we have faith in the salvation that God worked for us on a cruel and gruesome Friday afternoon nearly two thousand years ago? That was when, "while we were still weak, at the right time Christ died for the ungodly. . . . [R]arely will anyone die for a *righteous* person . . . But God proves his love for

"Work in Progress"

us in that while we still were *sinners* Christ died for *us*" (Rom 5:6, 7a, 8, NRSV). If we believe that, then the past is over and done, and we can get on with living and loving as people who know that we are free from the consequences of sin. Justification—being made right in God's sight—is an accomplished fact, not by anything that *we* have done, but trusting in what *God* has done. We can get on with dedicating our whole life to living out our gratitude for what God has done for us in Jesus Christ in words and deeds of compassion and mercy and courage and hope.

Paul points to some specific results of our salvation that God has already accomplished. We are no longer *enemies* of God. We have *peace* with God. Peace is more than just a cessation of *hostilities* with another. Peace is a bond of creative *harmony* between people, genuine reconciliation between adversaries. Many recent events have demonstrated that, though the Cold War is over, the United States and Russia are *still* not at *peace*. There is still mutual suspicion. There is still competition. There is still quickness to take offense. *Believers* do not simply have a *truce* with God, but genuine *peace*—and it is all *God's* doing. God has pronounced us fully acceptable, *not* through *our* keeping of the *law*, but through *God's* sacrifice of his *Son*. Remarkable! And really living in peace with God means living in peace with everything that God has *made* and over which God has *sovereignty—all of creation*. We don't have to *make* the peace—God has already *done* that. It has nothing to do with any efforts of our own. We just need to *keep* the peace God has given, to *enjoy* the peace God has created.

Paul also says that we exist in a state of *grace*. It's not just God's kindly attitude toward us. It is God's active role in our lives—undeserved love, undeserved care, undeserved provision for what we need. And we can even boast that we are created in God's *image* and destined for *fellowship* with God and therefore our firm hope is to be partakers in the *glory* of God—not sentenced to an eternity of shame, but free to exult forever in the fact that we are children and therefore heirs of the one who created the entire universe. And finally, we know the outcome of whatever suffering we may endure in this life; it cannot destroy us, it cannot defeat us, it cannot make us less in God's sight or signal that God has abandoned us. So suffering can only make us more like Jesus Christ, who suffered unjustly at the hands of some weak, silly, scared people who worked awfully hard at *denying* love and *rejecting* grace and dooming themselves to the *failure* of trying to *save themselves*.

I confess that, as a person of Reformed background, it always amuses me to be approached by someone and be asked, "Are you saved?" The implication is that there is something *I* must do for *myself* or that *they* are going to do *for* me. Paul was quite convinced that no person can possibly justify her- or himself in God's eyes, as Martin Luther and the other Reformers were also convinced fifteen centuries later. All *we* can do is to be open to the reconciliation that God has *already* achieved. Haven't they heard? The salvation is already accomplished—God has *already* made me right, blameless, and acceptable through the death of Jesus Christ. That's the good news. I need only trust the fact of what is already *true*. It is not a matter of jumping through any additional hoops. It is not a matter of discovering any additional truth.

But we mustn't think that an answer of "Yes" to the question "Are you saved?" is all that matters. Justification—being regarded as right, blameless, and acceptable—is not the final goal of the Christian life or the end of Christian experience. *Justification* is only the *beginning*. To be a *Christian*—to be so grateful for God's salvation in Jesus that we dedicate our lives to following and obeying Christ as his disciples—is to be always a work in progress. You and I can never assume that we have arrived at the fullness of what God intends for us to be. We should never think that we have become somehow worthy of Christ having died for us. We must never suppose that the Holy Spirit cannot bring us to a more perfect servanthood in the likeness of Jesus. That is what we declare our goal *is* when we say "Yes" to the accomplished fact of God's salvation. It may well involve hardships. But what God has *already done* for us is the source of our confidence about what God will *yet* do. This God who has already given us so much, freely and purely from an abundance of love for us, surely will not abandon us or betray our trust.

"Justification" means that God regards *us* as righteous. That is our faith in something that happened thousands of years before we were even born. But that is only the beginning. We discover, as we grow from our *justification* into *Christ-likeness*, that we are surrounded by God's mercy and supported by God's care. God's love becomes the central and determining motive in everything that we do, and we find ourselves in a new, deeper relationship with God who created us for that very purpose. We grow more "saintly," if you will, more "holy." And that process, which again is really no work of our *own*, but the inevitable work of the *Holy Spirit*, is known in the Bible by another technical word—"sanctification". It comes from the Latin word meaning "holy" or "sacred." It is the term that describes our living out the life that God has promised us who believe, of growing up into the freedom that God has given, of becoming more and more like Jesus every day of our lives as more and more we turn away from our *own* agenda, from self-love and from self-indulgence, to love for God that prompts us to serve others lovingly in the pattern of Christ.

I will not insult your intelligence by claiming that every Christian is growing steadily and effectively and devotedly into the likeness of Jesus Christ. Many of us have known people who, though they did *not* profess faith

"Work in Progress"

in Jesus Christ, were in fact *more* Christ-like than some every-Sunday worshipers. We have all known baptized people who have not moved beyond the "justification" stage, who, having heard of their salvation in Jesus Christ, failed to grow in love and hope, or other people who somehow think that they have arrived, fully and completely, and deserve specific privileges and claim certain prerogatives. And that is why, technical as they sound and boring as they may seem, these terms that Paul uses—"justification" and "sanctification"—are important to you and me. They keep us mindful that a Christian always *should* be, and, whether he or she realizes it, always *is*, a work in progress. The fact that we *are* not and never *will* be Jesus Christ does not keep us from striving to be obedient to all that Christ commands. The fact that Jesus Christ is *uniquely* the *Son* of God does not dissuade us from discovering all that it means for *us* to become *children* of God.

There came a time in Jesus' earthly career that it was appropriate to pass on and share some of his power and authority to preach and to teach and to heal. Jesus had many followers in the sense of people who sought him out to hear what he had to say and to claim his mercy for their sins and to present their ailments for his cure. They believed he had power to speak truth and forgive transgressions and perform miracles to help people. But Jesus needed apostles who would go out and minister to others he did not have time to reach, disciples to carry *on* his ministry of preaching and teaching and healing after his death and resurrection. He gathered twelve of his followers "and gave them authority over unclean spirits, to cast them out, and to cure every disease and every sickness. . . . [He told them,] '[P]roclaim the good news, "The kingdom of heaven has come near." Cure the sick, raise the dead, cleanse the lepers, cast out demons'" (Matt 10:1, 7–8a, NRSV). We can imagine that they were astonished and amazed that Jesus would give them such an authority and not a little apprehensive that Jesus would give them such an agenda. But we know from the testimony of the Bible that they found themselves able to do all that Jesus had commanded, by the power of the Holy Spirit, and to grow in their ability and their dedication, and, along the way, to grow in their understanding of God's loving purpose in Jesus Christ. They were, each one of them, a work of God in progress (even Judas Iscariot, until he *lost* faith), growing into the likeness of Christ Jesus their Lord.

Are *you* growing, maturing, becoming? Justification is merely the *door* to the life *for* which and *to* which God has saved us in Jesus Christ. It is the threshold of a new relationship with God and with others in which we experience God's love and God's peace. If we are grateful for what God has done for us, we move beyond being "acceptable" in God's sight to being an active agent of God's redeeming love in the likeness of God's Son Jesus Christ. Our

Eleventh Sunday in Ordinary Time

"forgiveness" ripens from simply getting off of the legal hook for our sins into the serenity of the relationship of parent and children, and the dedication of master and disciples, and the blessings of eternal life here and now. All of these together make up the fullness of what the Bible means by "salvation."

"Are you saved?" someone may someday ask you as you walk down the street or through an airport. I hope you respond, "Yes, of course; God did that two thousand years ago. *Now*, I am a work in progress."

Twelfth Sunday in Ordinary Time
Spanish Springs Presbyterian Church, Sparks, Nevada
June 22, 2008

Genesis 21:8–21
Romans 6:1b–11
Matthew 10:24–42

"God's Other Life"

In November of 1961, my father delivered the keynote speech at the annual meeting of the Southwestern Section of the American Association of Petroleum Geologists in El Paso, Texas. At the time, he was the exploration manager for El Paso Natural Gas Company. That year's meeting was a special international gathering of geologists from Mexico and other Latin American countries as well as the United States. The other major speaker at the meeting was Guillermo Salas, an internationally-acclaimed geologist who was then Mexico's equivalent of the secretary of the interior. My mother had an important part in the meeting, too—she helped organize events for the wives who came to El Paso with their husbands—remember, there were not many female geologists in those days, and many wives did not work outside of the home—planning tours to Juárez and so forth, and employing her artistic skills to design the program cover and make posters to put up in the lobbies of the conference hotels. For several weeks before the convention, my father worked diligently on the speech, crafting it with just the right words and practicing his delivery, while the tables in our house were covered with poster boards and bottles of India ink and dozens of colored pencils.

Twelfth Sunday in Ordinary Time

At the time, I was ten years old, just two months into fifth grade at Mesita Elementary School. Even at that age, though, I understood that this was a significant event for my parents, and a distinct honor for my father, and the speech was something very important to him personally and professionally. I don't know whose idea it was—my mother's or my father's—that I should be taken out of school that day to hear my father deliver his address. It was always a big deal when one of my fellow students was excused from class for something—even a dental appointment. So there was a buzz of attention when my mother came into the classroom to fetch me that day. My teacher, Mrs. McCreary, had been encouraging of my being present when my father spoke, and may even have said something to the class about it—I don't remember. I had occasionally been out of school for illness, but never for any reason other than going to the doctor or staying home sick. On those occasions, my experience of life outside of the classroom on a school day had been limited to sitting in a waiting room or being confined to bed.

I remember much about my father's speech. It focused on the dangers of reliance on foreign oil and gas exploration and production, comparing America's growing dependence on such energy sources to ancient Rome's increasing dependence on outlying provinces for its grain supplies (and we all know what happened to Rome). But one of my main impressions of the entire experience of driving down to the Plaza Theatre (which had been rented for the plenary meetings) and being surrounded by hundreds of adults was my astonishment that so much was going on in the city of El Paso on a school day. *My* world, Monday through Friday, nine months out of the year, was all within the schoolyard and buildings of Mesita Elementary School. There were rare occasions when I had some notion of the outside world during those hours—the cars whizzing by on Mesa Street during recess had to be going *somewhere*, after all, and I remember the times when my mother stopped by the school and hailed me through the chain-link fence at lunchtime recess to let me know that Alan Shepard and then John Glenn had landed safely from their space flights. But I was amazed to learn one day in November 1961 that the world was functioning, had a life totally separate and apart from and oblivious to what was going on at Mesita Elementary School.

I know that that experience was not unique to *me*. Most children make such a startling discovery at some point or another. But there is something about our basic egocentricity, as human beings, that renders us slow to appreciate the truth that *our* concerns and *our* activities are not the only things happening in the universe. And our limited vision as *children* sometimes survives or reasserts itself into our *youth* and *adulthood* and becomes a shared characteristic that affects us not only as individuals, but as families, as clubs,

"God's Other Life"

as companies and agencies, as communities, as nations, often as churches. It can lead to cultural or even spiritual myopia, even arrogance. Because we're *here*, we can't imagine that anything important is happening *there*. In fifth grade, I sort of assumed that everything going on at my house pretty much stopped when I left for school in the morning and didn't resume until I got home again. As far as I was consciously concerned, nothing much was happening in the whole city of El Paso between eight-thirty and three o'clock on weekdays except pencils writing on paper and chalk writing on chalkboards in the city's schools. And so I was fascinated, and maybe a little embarrassed, to see the city bustling that day as it never did whenever I might be downtown on Saturdays and Sundays. It had a whole 'nother life of which I had not really been aware.

As *Christians*, I think we are sometimes like *I* was as a *schoolchild*. We tend to assume that *our* experience of God is the *full* experience of God, the *only* experience of God. And that is natural, particularly given a certain interpretation of Jesus' words about being the way, the truth, and the life, and that no one comes to the Father except through him. We *do* affirm, with the New Testament, that Jesus is uniquely the Son of God, the fullest revelation of who God is and what God is like and what God desires and expects from us, and that salvation, wholeness, eternal life, can be had only by having faith in Christ.

But that theological affirmation is quite *different* from the assumption that commonly *accompanies* it that God's efforts toward salvation and wholeness and eternal life are confined to Christian history or even limited to the story told in the Bible. A little reflection on our part will confirm that God's saving activity is not restricted to what we read on the Bible's pages; it continued and expanded *after* the last word of the Bible was written, and continues *today*, among *us*, right *here*, for instance, not to mention historic events like the Protestant Reformation, and the opening of the church to women's leadership, and the Civil Rights movement and the integration of churches. And if the *history* of the saving work of God is *longer* than the period *covered by* the Bible, it only makes sense that the *scope* of the saving work of God is even *broader* than the events *chronicled in* the Bible. The fact that God chose Abraham to be the ancestor of a great nation that would be blessed by God and be given a special role in the redemption of God's creation does not mean that Israel is the *only* nation that God blesses, does not mean that God isn't interested in *other* people or that God doesn't *love* them, does not mean that God's great work of salvation and wholeness and eternal life doesn't encompass *other* cultures in God's great recipe for bringing to fulfillment all of God's hopes for the world that he formed and then clothed with vegetation and then created animals to benefit from it and then populated it with human beings of every race and custom and language, even religion.

The world's one-and-a-quarter billion Muslims point to the event reported in today's reading from Genesis as the origin of their faith. Ishmael, the son of Sarah's slave-girl Hagar, fathered by Abraham but not destined to be the bearer of the covenant, was sent out with his mother into the desert to die but was cared for by God and himself became the progenitor of a great people, the Muslims. Historically, that assertion requires a lot of qualification, since Islam did not begin until it was announced by Mohammed, who didn't live until the sixth century after Christ. It is probably not even an ethnologically accurate explanation for the Bedouins among whom Islam spread so rapidly once it *did* get started. But the story is an important corrective to the misguided belief that God cares only for the biological and spiritual descendants of *Abraham*. "As for the son of the slave woman," God said to Abraham, "I will make a nation of him also, because he is your offspring" (Gen 21:13, NRSV). And the Bible testifies that "God was with the boy, and he grew up; he lived in the wilderness, and became an expert with the bow. He lived in the wilderness of Paran; and his mother got a wife for him from the land of Egypt" (Gen 21:20–21, NRSV). When Abraham died, Isaac and Ishmael buried him together. Genesis tells us that Ishmael had twelve sons, the same number as the sons of Jacob, who fathered the twelve tribes of Israel. Except for some genealogical references, that is the last that Israel's Bible tells us about Ishmael. But if God was faithful to this promise he made to Abraham—and God's faithfulness to his *other* promises to Abraham makes *that* a *certainty*—God cared for Ishmael and his descendants, and reckoned them, too, into God's plan for redeeming creation.

Actually, that very term, "plan," is somewhat misleading. It is probably better to use the word "purpose," for "plan" makes it sound as if it's all drawn up in schematic form in some heavenly workroom, intolerant of deviations, impossible of surprise. Not everything that happens is necessarily according to a "plan," although God is able to and does use it to fulfill his *purpose*. For instance, God certainly is not a God who wills violence, though violence is a part of the history that the Bible tells. God is not a God who approves of deception, though Abraham used deception to preserve his and Sarah's life, as did his son Isaac, as did many other heroes of the Bible. And I don't think that we should accuse God of promoting jealousy, although the fact that God's directive to Abraham to send Hagar and Ishmael into the wilderness happened to coincide with Sarah's jealous ultimatum shows that God pursues the great divine purpose in, with, and under the twists and turns of human emotion. As far as the plot of the Bible is concerned, the birth of Ishmael was a rather irrelevant footnote to the tale, a mistake taken care of by sending him and

"God's Other Life"

his mother away with a loaf of bread and a canteen of water—hardly enough to see the boy through to the greatness God promised. But God does not so casually dismiss those whom he loves.

> When the water in the skin was gone, [Hagar the slave woman] cast the child under one of the bushes. Then she went and sat down opposite him a good way off . . . ; for she said, "Do not let me look on the death of the child." And as she sat opposite him, she lifted up her voice and wept. And God heard the voice of the boy; and the angel of God called to Hagar from heaven, and said to her, . . ."Do not be afraid; for God has heard the voice of the boy where he is. Come, lift up the boy and hold him fast with your hand, for I will make a great nation of him." Then God opened [Hagar's] eyes and she saw a well of water. She went, and filled the skin with water, and gave the boy a drink. (Gen 21:15–19, NRSV)

And, while the *Bible's* attention turns back to Abraham's descendants through *Isaac*, God is *also* busy fulfilling the promise God had made to Abraham about *Ishmael's* progeny becoming a great nation.

Do we think that God was not at work among the Egyptians, the Babylonians, the Greeks, the Chinese, the Romans, the Goths, the native peoples of North and Central and South America, the Pacific islanders, working out his purpose of bringing all of creation in line with his intention? The Israelites had done nothing more to earn God's favor than any of the other tribes and nations of the world. God selected them, without precondition, for the special blessing and privilege and obligation of being in covenant with him to obey his commands and bear a testimony that would constitute a blessing to all these others. But God did not *disparage* the others. God's ancient promise to Ishmael remains a contemporary theological reality; God's loving concern extends to the Bedouins of Muslim faith, as it does to *all* the peoples of the earth, *whatever* their religion. God does not perfect people before deciding to work through them to bring about God's purpose that is greater than one individual or one tribe or one nation or even one religion. God has a life *beyond* our seeing, *beyond* our knowing. God is at work among the outcasts and refugees of the world, the exploited and the abused, like Hagar and Ishmael. God has a concern *beyond* our horizon of interest. The God of the chosen people is also the God of the whole creation, including even people who have never seen the Bible or heard the gospel. God has a love *beyond* those who worship him as the commandments prescribe, including those whom we are accustomed to count as enemies and aliens, foreigners beyond our political and economic and religious borders and strangers to our ways of thinking and acting.

Twelfth Sunday in Ordinary Time

We have a responsibility to give witness to God as he has revealed himself in Jesus Christ. But we mustn't assume that what we know of God is God's only story, or the whole one. To do so is to put God in a box. That's what Solomon tried to do with the temple. That's what the Pharisees and the scribes and the chief priests tried to do with the cross. That's what some early Christian leaders did by insisting that Gentiles must be circumcised and obey the Jewish dietary laws. In each case, the insiders thought God had no life beyond the one they knew, no purpose that could encompass people different from themselves, no blessing that could claim them, *too*, as his own to be cherished and to be redeemed. The Bible tells of Israel's experience of and with God. But the Bible informs us, in telling of God's provision for Hagar and Ishmael, that God has a life beyond its pages.

I puzzled over my new knowledge of life outside of Mrs. McCreary's classroom, was amazed to learn about its existence, wondered why I hadn't realized it before. All of those people, carrying on their business, fulfilling their responsibilities, pursuing their interests! But at the end of my father's speech, my mother brought me back to Mesita School where, for the time being, I belonged, to learn the lessons I needed to learn before I became a part of that bigger world.

Thirteenth Sunday in Ordinary Time
Spanish Springs Presbyterian Church, Sparks, Nevada
June 26, 2005

Genesis 22:1–14
Romans 6:12–23
Matthew 10:40–42

"The Test"

Reverend Stephen McDermott stood in the recently-paved parking lot of the new church building, admiring the beautiful structure about which he had dreamed for so many years. It had been a long journey of ministry through several unexpected places, far from what he had imagined when he first sensed the call to enter seminary and then seek ordination. That was almost two decades ago, now, when he was a clerk in his father's grocery store in Campbellton. He had been to university, but when he graduated, his father had asked him to come back home to help in the family business. He had married the girl next door, literally—Sally Warfield—and they had settled down to a conventional life of husband and wife, assuming, though without much enthusiasm, that Steve would one day inherit the store, and their son, should they have one, would come to work at the store and eventually inherit it in turn. But the son had never come, even after fifteen years of marriage, then, and it seemed that, *now*, he never *would*. Steve's brother had moved away after attending university and entered the engineering field, clearly having no interest in the grocery business.

Thirteenth Sunday in Ordinary Time

It was on the eve of his fortieth birthday that Steve had received his sense of call to the ministry, clear and urgent. He had been praying, after reflecting on the minister's sermon in worship that morning about "Ask, and it will be given you" (Matt 7:7a, NRSV). What he had prayed *for* was guidance in deciding whether to *remain* in the grocery business, or try something *new*, recognizing that it would mean risking all that was comfortable and familiar. But Steve was just about ready to *take* the risk rather than committing himself to spending the *rest* of his life doing what he had done *all* of his life, and what his father had done all of *his* life *before* him.

His father, in fact, had retired and moved to Florida a year earlier, leaving Steve to persist, so he thought, in something that was more of a habit than a joy, more of a routine than a passion. And that very night, Reverend Andrews had called to invite him to attend a meeting hosted by the presbytery, encouraging people to consider ministry as a second career. The denomination was forecasting a shortage of ministers, and meetings like this were being held all across the country to ask people who had had some adult experience in business or other occupations to consider whether God might be calling them to ministry. Steve had interpreted it as a sign from God, and the very next week found himself sitting in the church parlor with a woman from the denominational headquarters and two others—a woman younger than he, who was a social worker, and a man somewhat older than he, an insurance salesman—discussing the looming threat posed to the church by too few candidates for too many pulpits. "We need bearers of the promise," the woman from the national office had said. "We need planters of the seed that will grow into a thriving tree." Three months later, Steve and Sally found themselves in a tiny one-bedroom apartment three blocks from the Broadview subway station, seven subway stops and a transfer from Knox College.

Over the years of seminary training, Steve had been a good student, managing to keep up his grades while working in a Sobey's grocery store two nights a week plus Saturdays. He remained true to his conviction that God was calling him to the ministry, and he and his classmates spoke of doing great things, preaching compelling sermons, teaching insightful classes, battling spiritual diseases, opening dull minds. But then, as graduation neared and he began looking closely at vacancies, Steve had been dismayed to discover that the majority of the church openings were quite small congregations in quite rural communities or struggling congregations in the inner city. That was not the vision that had come to him when he had discerned God's call. He would eventually serve in both kinds of churches—two in small farming communities, four years in the first parish and six years in the second, and then three years in a small financially-ailing church in an unfashionable urban

"The Test"

neighborhood where the people were aging even faster than the little brick bungalows. He had never preached to more than thirty people on a Sunday; had never had a class of more than half a dozen, whether it be children or youth or adults; had never saved a soul to the best of his knowledge, at least not in the way that makes a gripping story; had never fundamentally changed a single parishioner's mind about anything that really mattered. Each of the church buildings had been run-down, could hardly accommodate any new members even if there had *been* any. If he could just get a congregation with some enthusiasm! If he could just get a church building that would *attract* new people instead of *repelling* them!

Then had finally come the call that he had envisioned for so long but had virtually given up on—he had applied, had been interviewed, had been selected by the search committee, and had been approved by the congregation of St. Mark's, a two-hundred-member church in Woodbridge, a northern suburb of the nation's nerve-center. It was somewhat surprising to be selected to such a position at the age of fifty-seven, but the congregation had had what they considered to be a bad experience with a younger pastor who seemed a little too faddish and appallingly short on pastoral skills, and the committee felt that a "seasoned" minister was what they needed just now. When he had been invited for an interview, Steve had expressed the right balance of vision for reaching out to the community and encouraging congregational growth, on the one hand, with visiting and caring for those who were already members, on the other. The committee didn't even seem to mind that he and Sally had no *children*—he had suspected that that had disqualified him for some other suburban churches to which he had applied in the past, congregations in areas that were burgeoning with young families. There were plenty of children here, but his own childlessness had not been an issue, so far as he could tell. And it would, at last, be an opportunity to have the sort of house that he thought Sally had always deserved.

Sally had been remarkably patient over the years of moving away from home to attend seminary, and then the odyssey from one little church to the next and then the next, playing the role of the pastor's spouse with grace if not with comfort. She had never demurred, not even that night when he came back from the meeting with the woman from the national office and announced that he thought her appeal had definitely been an answer to his prayer a week earlier, when Reverend Andrews' telephone call itself had so clearly seemed God's response to his plea for guidance. Sally had been content, if not ecstatic, to be the wife of a grocer in Campbellton, where she had kept the accounts and occasionally helped at the cash register. She had been content, if not ecstatic, to work as a bookkeeper for the co-op in Chesterville and for the Busy Quill stationers' and office supply store in Seaforth and most recently for the Danforth Road recreation center. But Steve always suspected that his wife thought that he had not lived up to his potential, had never achieved what she had expected of him since the time when, as he thought, God had specially called him to be a minister. Whatever such thoughts she *had*, she kept discreetly to *herself*, not even objecting, in a prolonged way, at least, to leaving her family and friends behind in Campbellton.

The church building in Woodbridge had been adjacent to a large empty field that stretched away to the horizon in the 1960s, when the building was constructed. It had never been a very attractive structure, built in A-frame style, and the sanctuary could only hold about ninety people, which the Session had long felt was keeping the church from growing as it otherwise naturally would. Four years after he had arrived, and the town having become an architecturally anonymous part of the metropolitan sprawl but with a portion of the adjacent field still undeveloped, a realtor had approached the Session with an offer to purchase the church property with the intention of leveling the building and constructing a large retail outlet on it and on the contiguous vacant property; the realtor would even help the congregation find a location in a newer part of the suburb where a new church could be built. After initial reluctance to give up their accustomed address, and some reluctance at paving the way for yet another Wal-Mart, the members of St. Mark's had voted nearly unanimously to accept the proposal. Now, the new church building was complete, a beautiful and stylish brick structure with a tall steeple that was bound to attract visitors, with a much larger sanctuary, a fellowship hall almost as big as the sanctuary, a nice parlor, a spacious office suite, and half a dozen Sunday school classrooms waiting to be invaded by the younger generation, with even some money left over from the sale of the older property, so valuable had that land been to Wal-Mart.

It was Thursday morning, and the first service in the new building would be on Sunday, and the wrecking ball was poised to demolish the old church building on Monday. Steve McDermott's mind went back to the insubstantial white frame structure of St. Andrews Presbyterian Church in Chesterville, and the leaky roof of Knox Presbyterian Church in Seaforth, and the uninviting squat dingy brick structure obscured by overgrown shrubbery that he could never get anyone to do anything about at Morningside Presbyterian Church, two blocks east of Sherbourne Street. Now, finally, a place where his ministry could begin to thrive, only a few years away from retirement! He hoped that he had the energy to deal with the influx of parishioners that he expected and that, after all, God deserved. He walked over to his car and got in and drove to the old church building, where he would spend the day packing his books and

"The Test"

files for moving to his new study on Friday, and telephoning the dignitaries who were scheduled to be present for the Sunday inauguration of the new sanctuary to give them last-minute instructions about the worship service.

On Friday morning before breakfast, Rev. Stephen McDermott brought in the newspaper as usual. The headline on the front page of the *Star* caught his attention: "Woodbridge Community Services Centre Condemned," with a smaller headline underneath that read: "Homeless Shelter and Halfway House Left Out in the Cold." A quick glance through the first paragraph informed him that the only place for homeless families and recently-released low-risk ex-convicts and offices that dealt with emergency family needs in the entire northern section of the metropolitan area had been pronounced structurally unsound, and that authorities were insisting that the private non-profit operation be evacuated immediately. The center had long operated on the edge of insolvency, and had no funds to buy or rent a new facility. "We were the last chance for so many people," the director was quoted as saying. "Now these people have absolutely no place to go."

Steve had an idea. He sprang to the telephone and dialed Mike Stewart, the attorney who had been handling the church's real estate transaction—a church member whom he knew would not mind being rung up at such an early hour. "Mike, good morning. Steve McDermott here. Sorry to ring so early. Did you see the headline in the *Star* this morning? Is there any possibility of delaying the demolition of the old church?"

The answer, in brief, was "No." The deal was closed, the terms were set, and the attorney knew for a fact that the Wal-Mart people were unhappy to have been kept waiting so long as it was. They would surely not give up the old church property, even temporarily. "Maybe you could turn over the *new* building to them," the attorney said with a chuckle at his fine joke.

Steve McDermott did not laugh. "Well, thank you. See you Sunday," he said, hanging up the phone.

Once placed in his mind, though, Reverend McDermott could not get the attorney's words out of his thoughts. And the words of another: "Lord, when was it that we saw you hungry and gave you food, or thirsty and gave you something to drink? And when was it that we saw you a stranger and welcomed you, or naked and gave you clothing? And when was it that we saw you sick or in prison and visited you" (Matt 25:37b–39)? He had been part of a ministry team in seminary that visited such places and helped out from time to time, had seen the needs of the down-and-out, had felt compassion for them. He also knew the community well enough to realize that there were no available locations suitable for the purpose. The attorney's words haunted him. "Maybe you could turn over the new building to them."

"*No*," he said out loud, tears welling up in his eyes as the vision of his beautiful new church building rose up in his mind. "No-o-o."

"Why, what's the matter?" Sally asked with concern as she came into the kitchen. He held up his hand and shook off the question as he brushed past her and out the front door to the car.

When he reached his office, Steve McDermott telephoned the clerk of Session. "Debbie," he said when she answered the other end of the line. "We have to have an emergency meeting of the Session tonight. . . . Yes, could you call them to meet at seven o'clock?"

"Are you crazy?" one Session member demanded as soon as Reverend McDermott had gotten to the point about giving up the new building. "This is preposterous!" said another. "Over my dead body!" shouted another. "We believe in helping the poor, but what will become of *us*?" asked another, a bit more thoughtfully. "I think you should resign," said another. "Or get some counseling," suggested another.

In fact, he *had* considered resigning, if the Session should deny his request. But of *course* they would deny it. Why *wouldn't* they? Why *shouldn't* they? Maybe they were *right*. Maybe he *was* crazy. He was hearing the same words over and over in his head, as if he were going insane. "Lord, when was it that we saw you . . . ?" He simply could not get that passage out of his mind. Sally had finally broken ranks with him, too, when she found out about his intentions. What had she waited for all these years? What had *he* waited for all these years? Was he now going to sacrifice the one thing that had finally made it all even a little bit worthwhile?

"But the homeless families!" he replied. "And the people fresh out of prison!"

Sally did not say another word to him all night, but glowered at him with icy contempt.

On Saturday morning, Steve went to his old office to finish packing, whether for a move to the new church or for a move out of the ministry, he did not know. He did not hear the man come in the front door, but looked up from a half-filled cardboard box as he heard someone clear his throat. "Oh, I didn't hear you come in."

"I'm sorry to bother you. I'm Kenneth Roberts, a friend of Mike Stewart's."

"I'm glad to meet you," Steve straightened up and held out his hand. "What can I do for you?"

"Well," the man said, "I'm hoping that it's something we can do *together*."

Steve motioned him to the one remaining chair.

"The Test"

"Thank you. As a part of a larger transaction, I recently acquired the old Elmhurst school. Do you know where it is?"

"Yes," said Steve. "It's been vacant for a couple of years. I understand it's to be demolished and the land used for a townhouse complex."

"Well, that was one possibility. But it's never quite gotten off the ground. Mike called me yesterday afternoon and said you had been upset by the community social services building situation."

Steve nodded.

"And then he called me back this morning and said he'd heard you were ready to turn your new church building over, or resign."

Steve was embarrassed that the Session meeting had so quickly gained notoriety. "Well, that's not *exactly* how—"

"Reverend," Mr. Roberts interrupted him. "I am a man of faith, and I believe that faith is nothing without works, like the letter of James says. I was impressed by your conviction, and I got to thinking—I could afford to give that school away, but it would take money to remodel it for the purpose of turning it into a new community social service center. The layout would be perfect for their needs, but some things need to be adapted and fixed up. Assuming the city code and zoning people can be satisfied, I'd be willing to donate it, if you could help me find the money to do the renovation."

Steve McDermott staggered back against the wall like a man whose life had just been given back to him. And his thoughts quickly turned to the roughly $100,000 that the church had left over from the sale of the old building after construction of the new one. That would surely be a good start, which the church members could be encouraged to supplement in thanksgiving to God for the blessing of their new building. Indeed, the congregation could be proud that it had responded to the needs of the community and the most needy of their neighbors. "Mr. Stewart," Steve said as he came forward and grasped his hand, "I believe you are an angel sent by God." And he reached for the telephone and dialed the clerk of Session.

Sunday morning was festive, as expected, and not least because there were so many first-time visitors, many of them children. Large as it was, the sanctuary was filled, including dozens of new faces. The service went as expected, with various denominational dignitaries taking part. At the conclusion, Steve McDermott walked forward to pronounce the benediction, but, before speaking the familiar words, he had an announcement to make. "Grateful as we are to God for this wonderful new building, we are even *more* grateful to God for what it can make possible—a rebirth, a recommitment, a redefinition of our congregation. Long as we have waited for it, this building must not become an

Thirteenth Sunday in Ordinary Time

idol. Anything *other* than God is something *less* than God, even a church. As you know, we had some money left over from the proceeds of the sale of our old building and after the construction of this one. With additional dollars from our pockets, we could do something truly great. Let me tell you about an opportunity that our Session is putting before us . . ."

Fourteenth Sunday in Ordinary Time
Spanish Springs Presbyterian Church, Sparks, Nevada
July 6, 2008

Genesis 24:34–38, 42–49, 58–67
Romans 7:15–25a
Matthew 11:16–19, 25–30

"Will the Real Me Please Stand Up?"

"I can will what is right," said Paul, "but I cannot do it. For I do not do the good I want, but the evil I do not want is what I do" (Rom 7:18b–19, NRSV).

The children and young adults in our congregation may never have heard it or seen it, but the rest of us surely remember the program "To Tell the Truth," first on radio and then hosted by Presbyterian Bud Collyer on television back in the days of black and white. Three contestants appeared, and a statement written by one of them was read to four panelists. The point of the show was for the panelists to figure out, by asking questions, which of the three contestants was the person who had actually written the statement—usually telling about some unusual occupation or amazing feat or peculiar hobby that the person had. The contestant who had written the statement had to answer the questions truthfully; the other two contestants were free to make up their answers. After each panelist had indicated which of the three contestants he or she thought was the true person described in the affidavit, Bud Collyer would say, "Now, will the real Mr. (or Miss or Mrs.) so-and-so please stand up." And the three contestants would pass glances back and forth at each other for a few seconds to build up the suspense, and finally the true explorer or author

Fourteenth Sunday in Ordinary Time

or world rumba champion would stand up. "Now if I do what I do *not* want," wrote Paul, "it is no longer *I* that do it, but *sin* that dwells *within* me. So I find it to be a law that when I want to do what is *good*, evil lies close at hand. For I delight in the law of God, in my *inmost self*, but I see in my members another law at war with the law of my mind, making me captive to the law of sin that dwells in my members" (Rom 7:20–23, NRSV). Imagine Christianity's greatest missionary, Paul, confessing that his *inmost* Christian self did not always have the upper hand.

We can identify with what Paul seems to be saying here. We have all had experiences of blurting out a hurtful word which we cannot understand our reason for saying. Something just came over us, and in a split second, the harm was done. We have given in to some immediate urge uncharacteristic of us, which we knew at the time was not the right thing to do, and the wrong is done. We are people who have been baptized into Christ Jesus; we have said that the most important thing about us is that we belong to him. Everything else about us is secondary, everything else about us is not of the essence of who we are. Why, then, does the real "us" so often yield to the person we don't want to be? We regularly pray that God will lead us not into temptation and will deliver us from evil—which surely includes our own evil that we are capable of doing—and we may pray fervently that God will govern our thoughts and our tongues as well as our actions. Most of us, I think, know exactly what God wants of us, and we are also aware of how stubbornly we refuse it time and time again. And though we may be remorseful afterward, we repeat the same wrongs and offer the same excuses at our next opportunity. So we do the things that we know we should *not* do, and we do *not* do the things that we know we *should* do, and we may notice sometimes that we do not seem all that different in our thoughts and words and actions from a lot of people who do *not* profess to be followers of Jesus Christ. If we truly love Christ in our hearts, if we truly belong to Christ, then why do we keep doing and saying *un*loving and *un*-Christ-like things? Why do we *not* do and say *loving* and *Christ*-like things? How we would like the real Christian "us" to stand up and be recognized and lock our un-Christian characteristics up and throw away the key! Paul seems to have hit the nail right on the head. Help us, Lord, to keep the commandments! If we could just do *that*!

But, honest as that confession might be, the context of this passage within Romans indicates that Paul was talking about his keeping the law and *still* not doing what he *should*! As a Pharisee, he had tried and come very close to fulfilling all of the requirements of righteousness, according to the Ten Commandments and the hundreds of other laws of Moses. He had kept the blasphemy laws. He had kept the purity laws. He had kept the sabbath laws.

"Will the Real Me Please Stand Up?"

He had even persecuted the followers of that dangerous rabbi from Galilee who had *broken* the blasphemy laws and the purity laws and the sabbath laws!

And that is the irony that Paul squarely faced here, in this passage, and that Paul forces *us* to face! In his very zeal to *fulfill* the law and to find salvation through his *own* deeds and his *own* purity, Paul was a part of those who had killed the Son of God, and he himself started killing the *followers* of the Son of God, because they did not seem to take the law seriously enough. They said that Jesus had the power to forgive sins, and had given *them* the power to forgive sins. They said that Jesus had the authority to heal on the sabbath, and gave *them* the authority to heal on the sabbath.

The *appointed* authorities thought that they had solved the problem by making an example out of Jesus by crucifying him, but it had only made things worse; people began to say that he had been raised from the dead, and was sitting at the right hand of God in heaven! Everything was so nice and neat and controllable when there were rules, and those who *followed* them were *good* and those who *didn't* follow them *weren't* good and could be looked down upon as enemies of God and unworthy of mercy, divine or human. But, looking back upon his life as a Pharisee, Paul recognized that, though he had done all that the law required, he had rejected God's ultimate revelation of that law in Jesus Christ. By rejecting Jesus Christ in the days before he encountered him on the road to Damascus—Jesus Christ who had healed sinners and fed sinners and forgiven sinners, Jesus Christ who had enjoyed parties and at times seemed so very unspiritual, Jesus Christ who had talked with strange women and eaten with tax collectors and prostitutes and seemed so very unholy—by rejecting *him*, Paul had rejected God's will.

We do not know whether Paul was one of those who had criticized John the Baptist for being an ascetic moralizing old stick-in-the-mud, always wailing about repentance, but he certainly was alarmed that *Christ's followers* seemed unconcerned about the obvious dangers of proclaiming God's forgiveness as freely and joyfully as *they* did. As a Pharisee, Paul had pledged himself to do the *good* by strictly obeying God's law. But it was Paul's very devotion to the *law* that had led him to do just the *opposite* of the good! In striving to do God's will by upholding the *law*, Paul had persecuted the followers of the Son of God, so that his very intention to do *good* resulted in what he *now* recognized to have been utter *evil*. Sin had so taken over the law that it used the law as an instrument to oppose God's gracious will of salvation and wholeness—something for the Presbyterian Church to ponder in the wake of another General Assembly meeting that made headlines this past week.

Paul discovered that he had been caught in a dilemma. It was unknown to him until he had become a Christian. "So," he wrote to the Christians at

Fourteenth Sunday in Ordinary Time

Rome, "I find it to be a law that when I want to do what is *good, evil* lies close at hand" (Rom 7:21, NRSV). Paul's very intention to do *good* and *follow* God's will had actually led him to do *evil* and *oppose* God's will by persecuting Christ's apostles and Christ's church for not obeying the law. Apart from Christ, and Christ's power to break the hold of sin on us, we, like Paul in his Pharisee days, will only continue to bring about *evil* precisely through our *legalistic* attempts to *compel* the *good*. Even when we are successful in fulfilling the requirements of the law—the Ten Commandments and the rest of the Bible's do's and don'ts—we have not accomplished God's will. And the problem with the *law* is that it leads us to suppose that, by *obeying* it, we will have done what God *requires*.

That is frustrating, isn't it? So it was frustrating for Paul. "Wretched man that I am!" he moaned. "Who will rescue me from this body of death?" (Rom 7:24, NRSV). But Paul recognized that frustration is in fact just the right background for hearing the gospel—the good news. Self-satisfied people (and our churches have a lot of them) do not even know that they are in *need* of the gospel, or really think that they need God *at all*; only those who despair of their *own* power to do what is pleasing to God really value Jesus Christ, and a lot of *them* are *out there*, not *in here*. In a previous church, I spoke to a woman one day who had wanted to come there for worship, but when she got to the front door, she was afraid to come in, finding our building beautiful but imposing, thinking that perhaps she wasn't good enough to enter. "Thanks be to God through Jesus Christ our Lord!" Paul finally sang (Rom 7:25a, NRSV). For Jesus Christ shows us how to *fulfill* the *law* and to fulfill *God's will* at the same time, by following *his* law of *love*. Jesus demonstrates in his own life how *we* may please God and fulfill the purpose of all the commandments and rules and regulations, in his deeds, in his teachings, in his mercy, in his gentleness, in his love. The *law* remains the *same*—the yoke is still something which each of us must bear. But Christ bears it *with* us, and in *doing* so, he shows us what it means truly to *obey* God.

As a person baptized in the name of Jesus Christ, having publicly confessed myself to be his follower, enlisted into his discipleship, placing my life and my talents and my treasure at his disposal, the *real* me is principled but gentle, pure-spirited but forbearing, righteous but forgiving, heaven-minded but concerned for my fellow earth-bound creatures, holy but working to combat physical problems such as hunger and homelessness and injustice, a follower of the law but putting first loving God and loving my neighbor as myself. As a Christian, everything about me that is ungenerous, unkind, quarrelsome, hurtful, impatient, skeptical, unforgiving, mean, self-righteous, unloving, is *not* the *real me*. "I delight in the law of God in my inmost self, but," said Paul,

"Will the Real Me Please Stand Up?"

"I see in my members another law at war with the law of my mind, making me captive to the law of sin that dwells in my members. Wretched man that I am! Who will rescue me from this body of death? Thanks be to God through Jesus Christ our Lord" (Rom 7:22–25a, NRSV)! Jesus Christ, in his merciful and redeeming love, is the only one who can show us who we really are. Will the real me please stand up?

Fifteenth Sunday in Ordinary Time

First Presbyterian Church, Norfolk, Nebraska

July 15, 1990

Genesis 25:19–34
Romans 8:1–11
Matthew 13:1–9, 18–23

"The Promise in the Seed"

In Franco Zeffirelli's production "Jesus of Nazareth," there is a scene in which Jesus, early in his ministry, addresses a crowd, many of whom are listening to him for the first time. After speaking about the living, evolving nature of the law of God, Jesus tells the crowd that God wants to write the law on their hearts. A man jumps up and asks Jesus, either out of skepticism or disappointment or frustration at simply not understanding, "Rabbi, you said you have come here to give us the good news. Is this it—the good news? That the law is living, like a man?"

"The good news I bring you is this," says Jesus; "that your captivity is over—captivity in sin. God fulfills the promise that he made to our people Israel, and reconciles himself to man. God is coming to you. To all of you. Even the most wretched. Do not shut the door in his face."[1] Zeffirelli gives us the picture of a Jesus who was beginning to perceive that many to whom he proclaimed the good news would doubt it, many would misunderstand it, many would even be disappointed in it and shrug it off.

---

1. Zeffirelli, *Jesus of Nazareth*.

"The Promise in the Seed"

I think that it is no heresy to suppose that as Jesus' ministry progressed, he was often discouraged and even perplexed—discouraged by the need to repeat over and over the simple truth of the kingdom of God, and perplexed that his hearers could listen time and again and yet not understand; discouraged by the resistance among those who perhaps understood too well, and perplexed that the human heart could grow so cold and hard. He spoke in words that the simplest peasant could define, and yet which the most learned sophisticates distorted unfairly. He demonstrated by his actions a truth that authenticated itself in the doing, and yet which was met with criticism and accusations at every turn. He offered life so genuine and abundant that it could not even be measured in days and years, and yet those around him preferred to lose their souls in the pleasures and advantages of the moment. scripture itself tells us here and there that Jesus "marveled" or was surprised at instances of unbelief or refusal to comprehend. Yes, I think that Jesus must often have been discouraged and even perplexed. So it is not beyond possibility that the story that he told in this morning's Gospel lesson about the sower and the seed and the soils was something of an autobiography, a reflection upon his own experience of proclaiming the good news. And, by extension, it was a statement of what the disciples could also expect, ministering in his name.

The first part of the thirteenth chapter of Matthew is commonly referred to as the "Parable of the Sower." But close examination of the text reveals that it is not a teaching about the characteristics of the sower—what makes a good one or a poor one. In the autobiographical dimension of the parable, the sower is preeminently Jesus himself. It is more a comment on the soils upon which the seed is scattered—which type of soil offers the seed an opportunity to sprout and grow and yield fruit. But above all, it is a comment upon the seed itself, upon its marvelous ability, when it finds root in the right kind of soil, to produce a miraculously abundant yield. The focus of the parable is not upon the sower's skill—in Palestine, seed is broadcast indiscriminately upon the surface of the unbroken ground, and then plowed into the dirt. Some of the seed happens to fall on soil compacted hard by long years' passage of feet and wheels, susceptible to being blown away by wind or washed away by rain even before the plow can be applied, out in the open where it is plainly visible to hungry birds swooping down and snatching up the morsels. Some of it happens to fall on soil which is thin, with rock close beneath the surface, so that when it is plowed under, the rocks radiating the warmth of the sun cause the seed to germinate quickly but then provide no rootage, so that the young plants wither and die. Some of it happens to fall on soil thick with sprouting weeds, which take the moisture from the ground and choke off the tender young plants. But some of the seed falls on good soil, and produces a yield such as no Palestinian farmer could even imagine. The point is that the seed is good, and has within it the potential of fruitfulness beyond calculation, if only it should happen to be scattered upon receptive soil.

Jesus seems to have taught mostly in parables. He well knew that the divine truth which he had to proclaim was first and foremost something not so much to be explained as experienced; it was straightforward and plain, neither ornate nor esoteric. It was mysterious but not secretive, lofty but not exclusive. It was too wonderful for human words, and yet he did not *disparage* human words. So he used words to paint a picture of heavenly truth in earthly colors. Jesus was not the first to realize the power of story as a way to reveal the truth; there are parables in the Old Testament, and the rabbis of Jesus' own day frequently told stories as a way of making their point. Like the spiritual teachers of his own time and like the scripture authors before him, Jesus knew, as George Buttrick, then pastor of New York's Madison Avenue Presbyterian Church, put it, "There can be no logic to prove the spiritual; there can be only the prophet's opening of a window in the hope that clay-shuttered eyes may find it a 'magic casement' looking out upon the mountains of God."[2] By speaking in parable, Jesus provided his listeners such a window. For him, heaven was a perfectly obedient and loving life. Living in response to God makes all creation a sign of heaven. "Was there a forgiving father?" Buttrick asked. "[A]nother Father was more forgiving, though unseen! Did a shepherd brave the darkening storm to rescue his sheep that was lost?—another Shepherd was out on a more hazardous quest for His human flock!"[3] For Jesus, everything revealed the wonder and truth of God. "The tenderness on the world's edge when daylight fades, the green fire of the grass, and the manifold life of wistful humanity were the handwriting of the Most High. Ever patient with our filmy sight, He brought forth from His treasure things new and old; and, to show us that other world, 'He opened his mouth and spake unto them another parable, saying . . .'"[4] And we are left to ponder, with Milton, "[W]hat if earth/Be but the shadow of Heav'n, and things therein/Each to the other like, more then on earth is thought?"[5] "The real world to Jesus was not the seen world," Buttrick noted; "the real world was the unseen of which the seen is but the form. Heaven to us may be a dream of earth; but to Him earth was a broken and shadowy reflection of heaven."[6]

---

2. Buttrick, *Parables*, xxii.
3. Buttrick, *Parables*, xxii–xxiii.
4. Buttrick, *Parables*, xxiii.
5. Milton, *Paradise Lost*, 5.574–76.
6. Buttrick, *Parables*, xxi.

"The Promise in the Seed"

The early church puzzled, as Jesus himself seems to have puzzled, why so *many* people resisted the simple truth so stubbornly, or why others seemed to respond so eagerly but then within a few months or days or even hours went on living as though nothing had changed in their lives. Realizing that the fault lie not with the *seed*—the gospel, which in their own communities was producing marvelous results of compassion and love and courage and hope—early Christians began to criticize the fitness of the soils—the hearers. They allegorized Jesus' parable so that it became more an explanation of *unbelief* than a summons to proclaim the good news *despite* discouraging results. Without question, there is good reason for each of us to consider what sort of soil our *own* heart provides for the fruitful growth of God's seed. But do we not have a greater tendency to observe and comment upon *other* people's hardness and rockiness and weediness than to harrow our *own* field, to remove the rocks and condition the ground and pluck the weeds from our *own* soil? And do we not generally seem to grumble that so much of our effort at sowing is wasted on the poor soil around us, rather than thanking God for the privilege of being a sower in his field, and for the inherent and faithful goodness of the gospel of Jesus Christ?

The fact is, we cannot do much about the soil in the fields that Christ has given us to sow upon, but that does not relieve us of the obligation to scatter the seed, which was the task of Jesus himself and all of those who are his disciples. Why did the simple truth that he proclaimed and that we are called to proclaim in like manner only now and then find a receptive hearing? Why did not more people flock to look into heaven through the window which he offered, and which those faithful to him still offer? Why have two thousand years of preaching the good news and teaching about the love of God in Jesus Christ not made the world a more merciful and peaceful and loving place than it is? That's simply the way it was for Jesus, the most able sower of good seed, and that's simply the way it is for those of us who are less able but who are trying to sow the same good seed in obedience to him—scattering it on every sort of soil, not judging in advance where it will find root and grow to abundance, but leaving that to God, looking back now and then to discover that the seed has in fact miraculously sprouted and flourished to yield thirtyfold, sixtyfold, even a hundredfold in what we would have thought to be the most unlikely of places—a cold and uncaring personality suddenly enflamed with love and generosity, a sullen and sorrowful spirit suddenly exuding joy and hope, a self-centered and self-sufficient ego suddenly heedless of self and living for others, a timid and cautious tongue suddenly loosened to speak with courage and declare with confidence the liberating and redeeming purpose of God.

Fifteenth Sunday in Ordinary Time

His telling of the parable suggests that it was just such a realization of the promise in the seed, the potential of the gospel, that motivated Jesus to persist in spite of obvious hostility and indifference to his teaching, to remain obedient in spite of soil which so stubbornly refused a harvest. The treasures of God were given not to be hoarded but to be shared, not to be locked up for the righteous but to be distributed freely to those bound in sin—their own sin and the sin of others. That is the knowledge that helps every Christian endure in her or his vocation as a proclaimer of the good news of the gospel—the news that every person is being offered eternal life, that the gates of heaven are open, that the kingdom of God is at hand.

All of us who would be disciples of Jesus Christ need to know the truth that this parable proclaims, including most definitely those who have been called to ministry as pastors. We so often wonder what is becoming of the seed that we have been entrusted to sow; we are so anxious that it have the opportunity to grow and produce a fruitful yield of strong faith and good works; we are so apt to forget that the results are ultimately not dependent upon *our* doing. Some passing remark spoken in truth, some seemingly inconsequential deed of faith and kindness, might lead to some sure sign of the kingdom in someone's life. And what is true of pastors is true of all those who would proclaim the good news of the gospel.

So our Lord calls us to persist in our labor without ceasing and without complaint, counting each day as a blessing and each encounter as an opportunity for discipleship. We are to bear the gospel of love and life and forgiveness and hope cheerfully and unafraid, giving thought not to our safety or reputation but only to our obedience, excluding no one from the grace of God either by our judgment or by our sloth. The servant is not above the master; the disciple should expect no different response from the world than our Lord received, nor any better selection of soil upon which to cast the seed of the gospel. So our faith and hope cannot be in these things, but in the goodness of the seed—the good news that Jesus has called us to proclaim in word and deed, which is none other than the truth of God in Christ himself. The promise is not in you or me as the sower. The promise is not in the soil which is given to us as our field of labor. The promise is in the seed.

Sixteenth Sunday in Ordinary Time
First Presbyterian Church, Dodge City, Kansas
July 18, 1993

Genesis 28:10–19a
Romans 8:12–25
Matthew 13:24–30, 36–43

"Promise to a Coyote"

I don't know whether the people who dreamed up the cartoon character Wile E. Coyote selected the name after watching coyotes in a zoo, or whether they simply thought that it made a sort of rhyme that would appeal to children and then formed the character to suit. In many parts of our country, you might never actually see a coyote in its natural habitat, going about its normal behavior. Surely, the Navajos, in whose traditional stories Coyote is a frequent supernatural character, have long observed the habits of the dog-like creatures in their homeland of northwestern New Mexico and northeastern Arizona, and noticed that they are wily animals. *Ma'i*, or *'atsé xaché*, as he is known in the Navajo language, is a symbol of force and slyness and knavery—a shrewd trickster, mischievous and deceptive, disloyal and dishonest, sometimes cowardly and sometimes foolhardy, stubborn and persistent. When he wants something, he will not give up until he gets it. He flatters. He cajoles. He perpetually lives outside the bounds of acceptable behavior. He is an opportunist, easily and frequently switching allegiances depending upon the circumstances of the moment, so his word is untrustworthy and his friendship is self-serving. He is sometimes amusing. He is often feared. Always, his appearance is a bad omen, for Coyote invariably brings trouble in his wake. He is careless and disordered—just see how chaotically he threw the stars into the sky!—and he observes no rules. Any good that comes from what he does is by coincidence, not by intention. He is an irresponsible deceiver who will distort and chicane and charm. Beware of Coyote.

In Navajo lore, Coyote is irremediable and unredeemable. One always has to be on the lookout for this character who is the opposite of everything that Navajos admire in a well-ordered life and a well-ordered world. And yet, there is something puckishly appealing about him. Perhaps that is what makes him so dangerous to himself, to those around him, even to the gods of Navajo mythology; he is not their *equal*, but, in many ways, he is their *match*. It is as if, in the mythology spun around this desert canine, the Navajos were holding up a mirror to their own understanding of undisciplined humanity, which brings disorder to the whole creation, sometimes, so that it groans for redemption; which brings chaos to relationships, sometimes, so that they are no longer gracious mutual self-offerings, but self-serving maneuverings for power; which brings sickness upon the inner spirit, sometimes, so that it no longer trusts its Creator, no longer seeks to fulfill the Creator's purpose, no longer accomplishes any good thing. Beware of Coyote. To some degree, he is each one of us.

Does Coyote remind you of someone in the Bible? Someone whose very name means something like "usurper" or "supplanter" or "over-reacher"? Someone who grasped hold of the heel of his twin brother when they were being born, who took advantage of that same twin brother when he offered the famished lad a bowl of stew in exchange for his birthright as the firstborn, who tricked his own blind and aged father into giving him the blessing meant for his brother, who was himself tricked by his sweetheart's father into laboring double the bargained length of service in exchange for her hand in marriage but was so stubbornly set on her to be his wife that he stuck at it, but who then got even with his father-in-law, who wrestled with God to a draw as day broke, and was given a new name and a limp in memory of the occasion? Coyote reminds me of Jacob—a selfish, brash, self-serving scoundrel who had very little concern for family and apparently no concern for God—until, that is, fleeing from the wrath of his brother Esau whom he had cheated so profoundly, and in search of a wife from among his cousins, Jacob by chance came to the very place where Abraham his grandfather had received the promise of God that Abraham's descendants would *inherit* God's promise that Abraham would be the father of a great nation that would be a blessing to all peoples. And he "stayed there for the night, because the sun had set. Taking one of the stones of the place, he put it under his head and lay down in that place. And

"Promise to a Coyote"

he dreamed" (Gen 28:11b–12a, NRSV). He dreamed perhaps the most famous dream that anyone has ever dreamed, and, located precisely in the middle of the book of Genesis, perhaps the most important. He dreamed that there was a ladder, or a staircase or a ramp, leading from that place up into heaven,

> [a]nd the angels of God were ascending and descending on it. And the LORD stood beside him and said, "I am the LORD, the God of Abraham your father and the God of Isaac; the land on which you lie I will give to you and to your offspring; and your offspring shall be like the dust of the earth, and you shall spread abroad to the west and to the east and to the north and to the south; and all the families of the earth shall be blessed in you and in your offspring. Know that I am with you and will keep you wherever you go, and will bring you back to this land; for I will not leave you until I have done what I have promised you." (Gen 28:12b–15, NRSV)

If you and I have any sense of justice at all, we have to wonder why God decided to renew the covenant promise with such an impious scamp as Jacob—cheating his brother, making a fool of his father, full of the undisciplined selfishness that the Navajos identify with Coyote and that Christians of all nations and races regard as the opposite of Christ-likeness. If God rewards such a scheming *wretch* with God's faithfulness, then what point is there in *our* trying to be kind and generous to others and humble and obedient to God? And we can't escape the scandal of it by thinking that Jacob's imagination was running away with him, or that the dream was some Freudian bubbling up of suppressed longings and yearnings. "Jacob woke from his sleep and said, 'Surely the LORD is in this place—and I did not know it!' And he was afraid, and said, 'How awesome is this place! This is none other than the house of God, and this is the gate of heaven.' So Jacob rose early in the morning, and he took the stone that he had put under his head and set it up for a pillar and poured oil on the top of it. He called that place Bethel" (Gen 28:16–19a, NRSV), which means "house of God." You see, Jacob wasn't celebrating the fact that he had had a *dream* there. He was acknowledging that God was *with him* there, and that God was promising to *continue* to be with him wherever he went.

As far as Genesis is concerned, it was the first time that Jacob had even *thought* about God, certainly the first time that Jacob had ever *feared* God, and had shown *honor* to God. The only time previous to this that Jacob even *spoke* of God was as a part of his lying to his father Isaac in order to trick him into giving him, Jacob, the blessing that Isaac had intended for Jacob's brother Esau. But Jacob was now what God had to work with if the promise was to be kept, if creation was to be redeemed.

Sixteenth Sunday in Ordinary Time

And so God did—made a promise to a coyote. Jacob's dream marks a change in Jacob's life, forecasts the outcome of his fugitive quest. But Jacob is still an opportunist, still an impudent schemer. And in the *next* scene, he *bargains* with God, proposes a *deal* with the ruler and Creator of the universe, that if God would stay beside Jacob and protect him and provide food and clothing on his journey, then he would accept God as his God, set up a pillar at that spot to be a shrine to the Lord, and return to God a tenth of everything that God gave Jacob. I don't know what the *Navajo* word is for such an attitude, but modern *Jews* have a term for it—*chutzpah*!

Well, as for the justice issue, the Bible testifies over and over again that God's justice is never at odds with God's faithfulness, including God's faithfulness to the divine purpose of salvation, of merciful redemption of the world that God created and that God loves. Even those who are thoroughly in "the flesh," as Paul would say, those who are steeped in concern for their situation in *this* world, self-*serving* rather than self-*giving*, spiritually undisciplined and yielding on all fronts to their own desires and their own appetites regardless of the effect upon others and regardless of God's commandments, may end up being used by God to further God's purpose. Consider how God used even Judas Iscariot to work our salvation. And Jacob certainly was an individual who was living according to the *flesh*. But one night, at a place where earth and heaven touched, God broke through the pride and greed and even fear of this young man Jacob, so undeserving in so many ways, and renewed the promise that God had made to Jacob's ancestors. And Jacob became overwhelmed with the sense of God's presence and God's providence. We can almost hear him in the Hebrew equivalent of today's youthful slang, "Wow! Awesome! Sweet!" And *we*, thousands of years after the event, are *ourselves* awestruck that God would be present and vow to *remain* present with even such a one as Jacob, that God would make a promise to a Coyote.

If Jacob did not entirely abandon his deceitful ways, he nevertheless came to see his actions and his predicaments in a truer perspective, and a broader one. Somehow, he was engaged in a partnership, or a struggle, with God. It wasn't all about *Jacob*. It was about *God, too*, and God's sovereign and holy desire to bless all of creation through the means of Jacob and Jacob's offspring. Now, Jacob knew that *he* was not in control of his destiny. *God* was. Now, Jacob knew that what happens on *earth* is inextricably entwined with the realities of *heaven*. Jacob's own choices and achievements were of cosmic import. He *should* have been *humbled*. All we know is that he was *awestruck*. Perhaps his pluck was necessary to God's purpose, so that the sorting out of the wheat and tares in Jacob's character would have to wait until *after* God's purpose had been achieved in him. At any rate, his journeys and his commitments were

"Promise to a Coyote"

now imbued with a sense of vocation. Now he knew that *he* was the one who bore the promise that God had made to Abraham, that he was crucial to the fulfillment of God's purpose, that he, his marriages and his mating, were God's chosen way into the future of creation. God had appeared at the very moment in Jacob's life when he was most vulnerable, when he felt most alone, when he was most in need. God did not enter Jacob's dream in order to judge his behavior, but to confirm that he was the one chosen to carry on the promise that God had made to Abraham—the promise of a place, the promise of a progeny, the promise of a posterity, the promise of God's very own presence. And God kept the promise.

The future is in God's hands. From his resting place in the desert, apparently all alone for the first time in his life, but then discovering that he was really camped in the middle of the rush-hour traffic of angels at the very place God had selected for their meeting, Jacob could not see *how* God was going to bring about the future that was being promised. Jacob could not *force* it to happen. He had to *hope*. And *that* meant trusting in *God*. "Now hope that is *seen* is not *hope*. For who *hopes* for what is *seen*? But if we hope for what we do *not* see, we wait for it with patience" (Rom 8:24b-25, NRSV). And Jacob's hope, based on God's promise, gave him the patience to work for Laban, his uncle and future father-in-law, for a month, and then for seven years, and then for seven years more, to win Rachel. And the purpose of God moved a little closer to its fulfillment.

Your hope and mine is based on the sure promises of God—God's faithfulness to the loving goal that God has announced. The destiny of creation is redemption—God has said so, and uses even imperfect, rebellious, self-consumed instruments to achieve it, even Coyotes like Jacob, sometimes even Coyotes like you and me. Perhaps, after all, what is most required to be an instrument through which God's purpose can be fulfilled is that we awaken to God's presence with us, and be struck with awe. When it seems most unlikely, when we are most in need, when we have reached the end of our own wits and wiles, when we think we are all alone in a God-forsaken place in our lives, maybe that is where God is best able to draw up a chair alongside us and say, "I am the Lord, the God of Abraham your father and the God of Isaac. . . . Know that I am with you and will keep you wherever you go . . . ; for I will not leave you until I have done what I have promised you" (Gen 28:13b, 15, NRSV). And there, in the lonely desert of our deepest needs and our greatest fears, God makes a promise to a Coyote, and weaves us into the fabric of salvation.

Seventeenth Sunday in Ordinary Time

First Presbyterian Church, Ponca City, Oklahoma

July 27, 2014

Genesis 29:15–28
Romans 8:26–39
Matthew 13:31–33, 44–52

"Hidden Certainty"

When, hundreds of years from now, historians look back on our lifetime, I am convinced that they will consider what has happened during the past two decades in South Africa as among the most remarkable events of the age—not just the *end* of *apartheid*, but its peaceful *aftermath*. The magnificent restraint shown by black South Africans since apartheid came to an end and majority rule was instituted in that land has been one of the greatest examples of Christian witness since the time of the apostles. Though there is still vast economic inequality in that nation, and many other social problems, the appeals of Bishop Desmond Tutu and president Nelson Mandela that the former victims of oppression lay aside all thought of revenge for the long decades of injustice and brutality were stunningly courageous, and the people's commitment to build a better nation for *all* South Africans, black and white and Asian, has been mercifully noble. I cannot begin to hope that *I* would be so willing to forgive, were I in *their* shoes. The black South Africans have a great deal to teach this white American Christian about turning the other cheek, about peace, about reconciliation, about love, about hope.

"Hidden Certainty"

As you know, Linda and I attended the annual meeting of the Hymn Society of the United States and Canada a couple of weeks ago. It was my eighth, I think, going back to my first Hymn Society conference in Vancouver in 1999. The subject that year was global hymnody, and one of the main speakers was Patrick Matsikenyiri, an educator and musician then lecturing at African University in Zimbabwe, formerly Rhodesia, and the person who wrote our opening hymn this morning, "Jesu Tawa Pano." Among his other honors, Patrick was selected to lead the music at the Jubilee Eighth Assembly of the World Council of Churches just the year before, in 1998, and he continues to tour around the world with African choirs.

Zimbabwe, just next door to South Africa, is a country that has had more than its share of strife over the years since British colonialism ended—its own brutal version of apartheid, then civil wars. I remember that, at one point during the conference years ago in Vancouver, Patrick told of the occasion when he was confronted by a soldier of one side or the other in one of the conflicts. The soldier pushed a gun into his neck and asked if he was going to sing. I was reminded of the student who died at Columbine High School after one of the assailants there pointed a gun at her and asked if she believed in God, and of the ancient Jews in exile in Babylon who were derisively ordered to sing the "songs of Zion" for their pagan captors. Patrick did not know what would happen, other than that God would be faithful.

The soldier must have been satisfied with his response, whatever it was, or his attention was diverted, or something, but Patrick is alive today to tell about it all, a person who has come close to violent death himself, and who has grieved for friends and relatives and students who have suffered the tragedies of Africa. And in explanation of how the population of a continent can suffer so much and still be so vital and vibrant, how the victims of injustice can endure so much oppression and still have faith in the goodness of the God who commands us to forgive and to *keep on* forgiving, he said, "You see, we African Christians sing our problems away." "We sing our problems away." And it might have been just then that Patrick led us all in singing a Kenyan hymn, "Anaweza bwana"—"The Lord is able. / The Lord is able to save. / The Lord is able to forgive. / The Lord is able to keep us secure. / The Lord is able to deliver."[1]

"We know that all things work together for good for those who love God, who are called according to his purpose," wrote Paul.

> What then are we to say about these things? If God is for us, who is against us? . . . As it is written,

---

1. Barker, "Anaweza bwana."

Seventeenth Sunday in Ordinary Time

> "For your sake we are being killed all day long;
> we are accounted as sheep to be slaughtered."
>
> No, in all these things we are more than conquerors through him who loved us. For I am convinced that neither death, nor life, nor angels, nor rulers, nor things present, nor things to come, nor powers, nor height, nor depth, nor anything else in all creation, will be able to separate us from the love of God in Christ Jesus our Lord. (Rom 8:28, 31, 36–39, NRSV)

And so African Christians sing about the certainty of God's love and the certainty of God's forgiveness and the certainty of God's justice and the certainty of God's peace in Jesus Christ, and they sing their problems away.

It would be a mistake for anyone to think, on the one hand, that God overlooks such wickedness as apartheid or genocide, or, on the other hand, that Paul the apostle is just camouflaging *evil* things as God's *will*. By saying that all things work for good for those who love God, Paul is not just rationalizing the perpetuation of oppression and injustice or ignoring the real agonies of life. He isn't turning Christianity into what Karl Marx thought all religion is—the opiate of the people. Evil remains what it is, but by our faith in the goodness and love of God that we know and see in Jesus Christ, evil loses its power to defeat us. Health, length of years, fortune, even what *advertisers* call "happiness"—these things all become *secondary* to the joyful certainty of the triumph of God's purpose, pictured in the scriptural imagery as the coming of the kingdom of God. Those who love God have the power to *face* evil events with the conviction of God's steadfast faithfulness, even have the power by faith to *transform* them into evidence of the nearness of the kingdom and the certainty that God is at work redeeming the world. They have the gift of being able to sing their problems away—not avoiding them, not blissfully ignoring them, not escaping reality, but putting them in God's perspective, weaving the texts and the tunes and the rhythms of God's promises into the fabric of daily living. And the *power* of evil—call it Satan or call it inhumanity—has *already* been *broken* anytime you can sing in its face.

It is not a matter of personal strength or mind over matter or positive thinking. It is a matter of trust in the faithfulness of the God who created the world and loves the world and sustains the world, and who created and loves and sustains you and me. Left to our *own* resources, dependent on our *own* gauge of reality, relying on our *own* wisdom, we would more likely *give in* to despair and bitterness and the base instincts of revenge. But the very God who seemed powerless in the face of evil that led to the cross on Calvary raised Christ from the dead by the power of the resurrection. And this is the God who has decreed that *redemption* is the destiny of creation, and redemption is

"Hidden Certainty"

the destiny of creation *despite* injustice, *despite* disease, *despite* hunger, *despite* slavery—a destiny that we are convinced is so certain that it must commit us to work to *end* injustice and disease and hunger and slavery, even while we sing away their power to defeat the kingdom of God. For the kingdom, though hidden, though obscured, though invisible sometimes in the glare of headlines and the shadow of heartbreak, is certain, is growing, is even imminent. And all the world's hatred and unfairness cannot change that, as African Christians know, and surely many people in other troubled and war-torn lands, and even in the impoverished slums of American cities and the spiritual vacuums of America's suburbs.

Jesus spoke to his followers of the hidden certainty of the kingdom of God—the triumph of God's purpose, the redemption of God's creation. There wasn't much visible evidence of the coming of the kingdom of God in the Israel of Jesus' day. Roman soldiers committed atrocities in the land God had given to the Jews, there were seasons of drought and days of poor fishing, people got sick and died, widows and orphans went hungry and unsheltered, people of all classes too often were interested only in their own desires and their own pleasures. But for the *perceptive* folk—those who had *faith*—there *were* the compassionate deeds and the prophetic words and the hopeful attitudes of Jesus—here a leper cured, there a lame man able to walk, here a woman lifted to self-respect, there an old man reborn in his understanding, here an earthy fisherman suddenly courageous to cast his nets to increase the population of heaven, there a ruthless tyrant powerless to silence the truth that threatened his authority.

So the kingdom of God grows from something as tiny and seemingly insignificant as a mustard seed into a large plant that gives welcome refuge to even the most unlikely. So it is hidden and unnoticed like yeast in a bunch of dough, but the result is certain from the moment it is mixed together, and you may not even recognize, in the routine of other daily chores, that it is having an effect, but, inevitably, there it is, bread enough for all. Our anxiety does not hurry the process. Our attending to the other business of living does not slow it down. The fact that its progress appears as paltry and unimpressive does not mean that it is unimportant. The possibility that we cannot measure the growth with yardsticks and statistics does not make it any less real. And the fact that there is yet evil and suffering in the world, sin and death, does not render God any less faithful to the divine purpose of redeeming the world, but only makes its evidence still more wondrous.

A prosperous Christianity, a self-satisfied community, a hope built more on the security of *things* than on trust in a *promise*, may not be able to understand all of this, may not take it too seriously, may even mock it. The outcast,

Seventeenth Sunday in Ordinary Time

the poor, the oppressed, those with hearts burdened down by sin or backs bent over in suffering—those who, by all conventional wisdom, have *no* reason to sing a song of confidence and trust—they are the *very* ones who often seem to have the most patient faith in the coming of the kingdom. The parables of Jesus do not so much teach a particular vision of the kingdom, but faith in the God who is ceaselessly active in the beloved creation, whose Word is trustworthy and true, whose forgiveness is generous beyond measure and whose love never ends, whose purpose cannot be defeated. The kingdom is a gift of God, unearned and uncoerced, for which those who love God will willingly surrender everything of worldly value and for whose coming they will gladly labor to remove every obstacle. Though it may be hidden from human view, those who trust in *God* live in its certainty day by day. "For I am convinced that neither death, nor life, nor angels, nor rulers, nor things present, nor things to come, nor powers, nor height, nor depth, nor anything else in all creation, will be able to separate us from the love of God in Christ Jesus our Lord" (Rom 8:38–39, NRSV). And to all of this, the church of Jesus Christ gives witness in the life and faith of the people of God worshiping, praying, and working together both in places of safety and in places of persecution, both in times of privilege and in times of suffering, in Africa, in Asia, in Latin America, in the Pacific, in Europe and North America, in large cities and tiny hamlets, in great cathedrals crowning public plazas with spires and stained glass and in modest meeting houses sprouted in forest clearings with thatched roofs and no walls at all.

Patrick Maytsikenyiri shared with us at that conference many examples of how the African Christians sing their problems away—words and rhythms and chords unfamiliar to North American ears, but words and rhythms and chords that *we need to hear.* They help us to appreciate more fully the broad dimensions of the coming kingdom of God, the colors and languages and perspectives. But, in fact, the songs of Christians from every culture, including our own, capture to some degree the very certainty of the kingdom of God which, though it may be *hidden* from our *eyes,* is God's own promised reality. More than a century ago, a Baptist minister by the name of Robert Lowry wrote these verses for a Sunday school hymn (the Hymn Society sang them during our final gathering for morning prayer at that conference several years ago, and we will be singing them at the conclusion of our service today):

> My life flows on in endless song,
> > above earth's lamentation.
> I catch the sweet, though far-off hymn
> > that hails a new creation.

"Hidden Certainty"

Through all the tumult and the strife,
    I hear that music ringing.
It finds an echo in my soul.
    How can I keep from singing?

What though my joys and comforts die?
    The Lord my Savior liveth.
What though the darkness gather 'round?
    Songs in the night he giveth.

The peace of Christ makes fresh my heart,
    a fountain ever springing!
All things are mine if I am his!
    How can I keep from singing?

(Refrain) No storm can shake my inmost calm
    while to this rock I'm clinging.
Since love is Lord of heav'n and earth,
    how can I keep from singing?[2]

---

2. Lowry, "How Can I Keep from Singing?"

Eighteenth Sunday in Ordinary Time
First Presbyterian Church, Ponca City, Oklahoma
August 3, 2014

Genesis 32:22-31
Romans 9:1–5
Matthew 14:13–21

"The Crippling Victory"

One day thirty-seven years ago, lying in a hospital recovery room, I heard a voice saying, "Bruce, wake up. Bruce." I opened my eyes and shut them, and opened them again to see the blurred image of Dr. McCarthy looking down at me. "It's over, Bruce. We had to take it all." "It" was my thyroid. Six weeks after noticing a swelling at the side of my neck, I was wheeled into an operating room and emerged more than six hours later, less my thyroid and several lymph glands, which, according to biopsies made during the surgery, were cancerous.

    In my medicated state, I don't think that the word "cancer" finally broke into my consciousness until the third day after surgery. That was the day when a consulting physician looked in on me, or rather looked in on my chart and my incision, and as he was leaving, casually said to me, "Many people live as long as five years after this kind of surgery." My father, who was present in the room, physically threw the man out of the hospital. I suppose that his words were *intended* to be *comforting*. As you can perhaps imagine, they actually had a much *different* effect. For those few words plunged me into a long night's struggle with fears and anxieties such as I had never known. In twenty-six

"The Crippling Victory"

years of life, I had never been admitted to a hospital or seen the inside of an emergency room. Now it seemed as if my death-watch had begun. In terms of the clock and the calendar, my long night's struggle was relatively brief; my family, my friends, and my church surrounded me with an experience of God's own love so great, so broad and so deep, that it mattered not whether I lived five *years* or five *hours*, each moment was so filled with blessings. My faith, but even more the faith of so many people around me, pulled me back into the daylight.

I do not know how I developed the malignancy—I do not believe that God is the author of illness and pain and suffering. More likely it was the devil. More likely still, it was the result of blind environmental forces at work in a fallen creation, an imperfect world—in this case, the madness of the Cold War. In my early childhood, we lived downwind from the Nevada nuclear test site. But in the course of struggling with my fears and anxieties and questions of why *I* had been thus afflicted in the prime of young adulthood, and how or whether I was going to live, I discerned, while trying to make sense out of life and death and illness and mortality, that the one I was struggling with was none other than God. And I became aware of my great blessing of the love that was being poured out to me from so many sources, and I recognized the eternity in each moment. I came away from the experience a different person in many ways—more sensitive, I think, to people who are ill and are faced with their own limitations; more conscious, I think, of the manner in which God blesses us in what the world would call "small ways," but which hallow creation daily; more understanding that "eternity" has nothing to do with the human calendar and historical time measured in minutes, hours, days, and years; hastened toward the decision finally to enter seminary rather than continuing to put off that commitment. These things I know yet imperfectly—sensitivity, the blessings of everyday, the eternity of the moment, the importance of taking risks—but I understand them far better *now* than I did *before* my episode of cancer. And they give me a much better ability than I had *before* to meet all of God's children with respect, with sympathy, with a sense of common humanity which was blessed in God's incarnation in the person of Jesus Christ.

Many of you, I know, have had similar experiences of perceiving God at work in the midst of personal crisis of illness, loss of a job, the death of a loved one, or divorce. Some of you are in the midst of a struggle *now* to discover the face of God upon that with which you are wrestling in the dark, demanding a *blessing* before you will limp away, lamed in body or wounded in emotions as a token of your struggle. The blessing of God, it seems, frequently comes at the cost of a *limp*.

Eighteenth Sunday in Ordinary Time

Few stories from the Old Testament can match the account of Jacob's struggle with the mysterious stranger for ability to spark the imagination. Who *was* the shadowy figure who steadfastly would not give up his name, but who ultimately yielded his blessing upon Jacob? What great *meaning* is captured in the change of Jacob's name to "Israel"? What sort of victory is it that leaves a person *crippled*?

The people of ancient Israel seem to have discerned in Jacob's nocturnal conflict something of their own experience with God. They interpreted their history as a nation as having been engaged in a struggle with God until the breaking of the day, contesting their national personality and resourcefulness against the divine will and purpose. In the course of going about what it thought was its own worldly business of politics and wars and legal codes and social activity, Israel found itself confronted with obstacles, strove for mastery *over* them and sought some sign of promise *within* them, and looked back upon those incidents to discern that it was *God* who had been their *real* contestant, molding the nation of Israel according to the divine will, chastening the people, making his presence known, putting heaven's claim upon all facets of the national life. And whatever national limp with which the people of Israel came away from their experience, they regarded as something of a *blessing*—a reminder that they had met *God* in a battle of *wills*, had matched *theirs* against *his*, and had come away *undefeated*, and yet *lamed*—*unbeaten*, but *changed*. But the episode of Jacob at the Jabbok, while telling of a nation trying to understand its history, also speaks to us on an *individual* level of human autonomy and the will of God, of testing, of wrestling with anxieties in the dark nights of the soul, and of discovering the face of God upon our crisis.

The same Jacob who, fleeing the murderous rage of his brother, stopped to rest for the night at a nowhere-in-particular place in the desert and there received a revelation of God, we now find returning to Canaan as God had promised him. He has learned that Esau is coming to meet him with a company of four hundred men. Still fearing Esau's anger, Jacob has cleverly sent on ahead gifts of cattle and donkeys in hope of appeasing him.

> The same night he got up and took his two wives, his two maids, and his eleven children, and crossed the ford of the Jabbok. He took them and sent them across the stream . . . Jacob was left alone; and a man wrestled with him until daybreak. When the man saw that he did not prevail against Jacob, he struck him on the hip socket; and Jacob's hip was put out of joint as he wrestled with him. Then he said, "Let me go, for the day is breaking." But Jacob said, "I will not let you go, unless you bless me." So he said to him, "What is your name?" And he said, "Jacob." Then the man

"The Crippling Victory"

said, "You shall no longer be called Jacob, but Israel, for you have striven with God and with humans, and have prevailed." Then Jacob asked him, "Please tell me *your* name." But he said, "Why is it that you ask my name?" And there he blessed him. So Jacob called the place Peniel, saying, "For I have seen God face to face, and yet my life is preserved." The sun rose upon him as he passed Penuel, limping because of his hip. (Gen 32:22–23a, 24–31, NRSV)

And Jacob lifted up his eyes and looked, and saw Esau running to meet him, and Esau "embraced him, and fell on his neck and kissed him, and they wept. (Gen 33:4b, NRSV)

Here are two very different encounters, side by side—one, Jacob contending with the man at the Jabbok, and the other, Jacob reconciled with his brother Esau—different, and yet, in the mind of the author, somehow related in an important way, as if the *reconciliation with Esau was dependent upon the struggle with the stranger.*

All through his youth, Jacob had been the crafty schemer. He was a master of deception. His character, it seems, still left much to be desired when he arrived at the Jabbok, about to cross over into Canaan to establish God's people in the promised land. Still the great planner, he prepared to appease Esau's anger by sending gifts to him. But in the course of carrying out his scheme, he was assaulted by a mysterious presence. He emerged from the struggle undefeated, but physically lamed; unbeaten, but with a different name. He also emerged with a blessing. He was, in fact, a new person after this encounter—the struggle at the Jabbok marks the change from the trickster to a patient, kindly man very much different from the Jacob of younger years, no longer the deceiver, but the venerated father of a nation; no longer the self-centered and over-indulged rascal, but the bearer of God's covenant. During the course of his wrestling, the personality of Jacob yielded to the bestowal of a new identity. No more would he be known as Jacob, the "supplanter," but as Israel. Perceiving that his encounter had been with God himself, he called the place Peniel, meaning "the face of God."

We are not told clearly who Jacob's antagonist was. Walter Brueggemann, one of the most insightful biblical scholars of our day, suggests that it is important that *we* are *not* told the identity of the man, and that *we* do *not* see his face, for this episode is intended to have about it a tone of *dread*. Jacob must have eventually determined that it was God himself, for he pressed the stranger for a blessing. But if it *was* God, it was not the side of God that we see clearly in the daylight, but the dimension of God that is inscrutably shrouded in holy sovereignty and neither to be appeased nor even found out. This is God coming to Jacob in the dark night of his soul, on the eve of a dreaded meeting with the brother whom he had wronged and who had vowed vengeance. This is God coming to Jacob when his fears and anxieties are at their peak. The unexpected encounter with the unknown antagonist is cast in the shadow of looming crisis. The two wrestle all night—neither one can quite have his own way. The contest is a draw, but the mysterious stranger, although compelled to give up a blessing, never divulges his identity, never surrenders his sovereignty. Jacob, although physically impaired, holds his own against the divine, but nevertheless emerges from the struggle changed in name. *Jacob* has *died*. *Israel* has been *born*.

God had chosen Jacob for a special mission in the fulfillment of his divine purpose, perhaps for some of the very qualities of tenacity and strength and self-confidence that Jacob exhibited in this struggle. If God was *testing* Jacob, God found him to be an extraordinary man, capable of bearing the weight of the covenant upon his shoulders. Yet *Jacob* learned that one cannot emerge from an encounter with God unchanged and unhumbled. During the course of the night, Jacob soared to bold heights, but then was corrected with a limp as he was taught that only *God is God*. The limp would ever after be a memorial of the night that he had *wrestled* with God, but it would also be a reminder of his *blessing*. He emerged from the experience with a new identity. And so Jacob, now Israel, comes to his brother Esau changed, with new grace given him by God. And having contended with God, he is prepared to risk the difficult task of being reconciled with his brother. When the daylight comes, as Brueggemann observes, the stranger is gone, and so is Jacob. Only *Israel* remains, a new person blessed and born in the struggle where he probed the identity of God. God stopped short of revealing his name—his hiddenness, his holiness, his mystery were intact. God remains God, but Jacob becomes Israel. And Israel must now be on the way to meet his brother.

Frederick Buechner refers to the struggle at the Jabbok as "the Magnificent Defeat,"[1] "magnificent" because Jacob proved an even match for the divine antagonist, "defeat" because he was made to limp. Walter Brueggemann prefers the term "the Crippling Victory"[2]; Jacob *did* gain a *victory* in wresting a blessing from the stranger, but at the cost of a *limp*, which every day thereafter proclaimed to others and reminded Jacob that there are no untroubled victories with the Holy One. The discovery that we are in God's presence comes not with gain of earthly riches, a satisfying family life, or enjoyment of good health. Even *non-believers* can be, and many of them *are*, healthy, wealthy, and reasonably satisfied. But we who accept Christ as Lord are privileged to become New Creations reborn in the image of God.

1. Buechner, *Magnificent Defeat*.
2. Brueggemann, *Genesis*, 270.

"The Crippling Victory"

It is not only dishonest, but also unscriptural, to suggest that new life can be had without paying a cost, or that one can be blessed with a new name—a new identity—without risking the *old* person, and even life itself, in a struggle with the divine will. For the image of God that is the measure of our newness was made clear in the person of Jesus Christ, who was crucified, who cried out in the depths of agony, "My God, my God, why have you forsaken me?" (Matt 27:46b, NRSV), and who, after three days, was glorified in the resurrection. Jesus knew what was involved in the long night's struggle in Gethsemane and on the cross. He learned of the risks inherent in the call to new life as he was summoning disciples and preparing them for what *they* could expect to encounter as his *followers*. Jacob's discovery at Bethel—"Surely the Lord is in this place!" (Gen 28:16b, NRSV)—is as much a *warning* to those who *fear* the insecurity of becoming a new person, the potential of having to endure a crippling struggle as a person of God, as it is a gracious *invitation* to those whose love of God prompts them to respond obediently to the call of Christ. But there is a blessing to be gained, even if it means death itself. As Jacob learned, as Israel came to understand, God, in the course of working out his purpose, sometimes permits an assault upon those on whom he depends, but, in the course of their struggle, grants them the inestimable blessing of seeing his face.

The Christian, Paul wrote, is someone who has *died* as *Christ died*, and has *risen* as *Christ rose*. Resurrection requires a crucifixion; new life requires a dying to the old. And it may be that in order to win the blessing, we must wrestle with God through some long, dark night, urgently asking the name of our assailant, seeking to discern who God is and how we can unveil God's holy mystery; and our emerging from the encounter lame, but new beings, humbled, yet more sensitive, finally ready to meet our brothers and sisters and to be reconciled with them. Whatever makes us more aware of others, whatever equips us better to be disciples of our Lord, whatever brings us closer to fullness in the stature of Christ, the very image of God, is a blessing. Any crippling struggle which brings us closer to complete obedience to Jesus is a *victory*.

Nineteenth Sunday in Ordinary Time
First Presbyterian Church, Dodge City, Kansas
August 8, 1993

Genesis 37:1–4, 12–28
Romans 10:5–15
Matthew 14:22–33

"Why Fear the Wind?"

"And after he had dismissed the crowds, [Jesus] went up the mountain by himself to pray. When evening came, he was there alone, but by this time the boat, battered by the waves, was far from the land, for the wind was against them. And early in the morning he came walking toward them on the sea" (Matt 14:23–25, NRSV). Of all the miracle stories in the Gospels, this one seems the most tempting to try to explain or to explain away. Both people of Christian faith and people of no particular faith offer such suggestions as, "Maybe Jesus was walking on a shoal, or even on the beach; from where the disciples were, out in the boat, it only *appeared* that he was 'walking on water.'"

But trying to reason such stories as this within the laws of physics is really rather pointless. It only diverts our attention away from what the evangelist wanted readers to understand. Writing for a church buffeted by storms of persecution and dissension, the evangelist had no interest in speculating upon the *mechanics* of the miracle. Matthew's concern was to show Christ's faithful lordship for those who trust and seek to follow him. In the episode of walking on the sea, according to Matthew, Jesus was not speaking *to* or offering a demonstration *for* people in *general*, but for the *disciples* in *particular*—not for

"Why Fear the Wind?"

the public at large, but specifically for his own followers, caught in the midst of a blustery gale that whipped up the waters into threatening waves. And the early listeners could easily see in the predicament of the disciples being tossed about in a little boat on a stormy lake an analogy to themselves, the infant church, menaced by hostile government officials and zealous defenders of Judaism and perhaps even by careless teachers among their own number, wondering whether the little craft would safely reach its destination with its precious cargo of believers intact. Like the disciples in the story, the people of the early church had been launched at Jesus' direction, but Jesus was not physically present in the boat with them; he had been crucified, and in spite of his glorious resurrection, the believers felt themselves to be adrift and at risk without the comforting assurance of Jesus to captain them to safety.

What did it mean to these early Christians that the first disciples had seen from their boat what they originally thought was an apparition, a ghost, walking on the sea, but then heard the figure in the distance calling to them, saying, "Take heart, it is I; do not be afraid" (Matt 14:27b, NRSV)? What did they think about Peter willingly stepping out of the boat at Jesus' command and walking toward Jesus on the water? What did they learn from Peter beginning to sink when he became frightened, crying out, "Lord, save me!" and Jesus immediately reaching out his hand and catching Peter and saying to him, "You need more faith, Peter—that's why you began to sink. Why did you doubt?" And how did it impress them that the disciples thereupon worshiped Jesus and proclaimed him to be truly the Son of God? Surely, they recognized Matthew's intention in telling this story; if, on a dark night of fear and helplessness, Christ had come to the aid of his first disciples, performing the miracle of walking on the sea, and had invited *them*, in the person of Peter, to perform the *same* miracle, then Christ was also available to help the struggling young church overcome the fearsome storms raging at its door and learn afresh the truth that its Lord was the very Son of God, master of wind and waves, master of fears and doubts, reaching out his hand to grasp even those faltering with half a faith.

One of the things that I find especially interesting about the story is that Peter, having shown *perfect* faith that, at Jesus' command, he *himself* could perform the *very same* miracle as Jesus—that of walking on the sea—was doing splendidly at it until he was distracted by the strong wind. *That* is when Peter the disciple became frightened and began to sink—*not* while Peter was performing the amazing feat of walking on water, but when he thought about the *wind*—when, we may suppose, Peter became conscious of the waves that were rising higher above him and threatening to overwhelm him. Now think of that—he had been fully willing to accept the miraculous fact that Jesus was

Nineteenth Sunday in Ordinary Time

walking on the water, and the even *more* miraculous fact that Jesus had empowered *him* to walk across a lake! One would think that Peter would have been too frightened to climb out of the boat to begin with, if he was fearful at all. But Peter *begged* Jesus to command him to do the *impossible*, and when Jesus did so, Peter willingly, even eagerly, complied. Why in the world, then, should Peter have been so terrified by the *wind* that he suddenly was in danger of drowning? "You of little faith" (Matt 14:31c, NRSV), Jesus chided him. The phrase could be aptly translated, "You half-believer!"—accepting without question your ability to walk on water, but not believing that you can possibly withstand the force of the wind. "[W]hy did you doubt?" (Matt 14:31d, NRSV). But by the time he said that to Peter, Christ, not disparaging even the *slightest* measure of faith, had already reached out his hand and caught him, and when they both got into the boat, the wind ceased. The disciples and their Lord continued across the lake, coming to land at Gennesaret, and there Jesus healed many who were sick.

Matthew puts this incident directly after the feeding of the multitude with five loaves and two fish, when the disciples had seen no possibility of satisfying the crowd with such seemingly paltry fare, but, in fact, "[a]ll ate and were filled; and they took up what was left over of the broken pieces, twelve baskets full" (Matt 14:20, NRSV). Now, one would think that the disciples would have been getting used to Jesus' ability to perform miracles, and they would have begun taking seriously his teaching that *they* start doing the *same*. It was the very nature of Jesus and his ministry. And when Jesus had miraculously walked on water and given Peter the spontaneous confidence to do so, he went on to work more miracles of healing on the other side of the lake. When were the disciples ever going to learn to trust his word, and to have faith in his power? When were the disciples ever going to learn to give up reliance on their own unimpressive credentials, and to realize that God's ability to work miracles *through* them was limited only by their lack of faith? Even Peter learned so little from the episode on the lake that his faith faltered again, badly, when Jesus was arrested and tried and crucified. But it was not just *Peter* who had a half-faith; the same was true of *all* of those first disciples. They could not appreciate the miracle that had already happened in their lives—the trust that they already had in Jesus that enabled them to leave their nets and their tax office and their families and their friends to travel with him around Palestine for almost three years, suffering ridicule sometimes, being threatened sometimes, not knowing where their next meal would come from most of the time, uncertain of the result of their wayfaring nearly all of the time. That was a major triumph of faith. And yet, when it came to a rather minor thing like feeding a hungry crowd, or curing a stubborn disease, or showing

"Why Fear the Wind?"

mercy to the outcast, they doubted, they mumbled excuses, they turned their eyes away from Jesus.

The same was true of the early church, it seems. Those first Christians had already *mastered* the miracle of *walking on water*. The truly *extraordinary* had become a *way of living*—that people from every walk of life, every race and nationality, would come together to worship the same God and eat at the same table and care deeply for one another—love one another so purely and so unconditionally that their neighbors remarked on it as being beyond explanation in the natural state of things. But when the wind came up and blew the waters into waves, when persecution threatened reputation and life and property, or when variant teachings disrupted the peace of the church and hard times challenged its mission, many wilted before the blast, not believing, in the absence of Christ, that God's purpose for the church was established beyond all human obstruction. Too often, their working assumption, in spite of all the evidence at their fingertips, was that everything depended upon their own feeble resources, which they must hide away securely or all would be lost, as if God could not safeguard his own.

More and more, the same seems to be true of the church *today*. God has preserved it for two thousand years—this body which by all logic should have been wiped out by the forces of imperial pride and jealousy or private greed and fear within a generation or two, which by all odds should have succumbed to the corruptions and abuses of the Dark Ages, which, according to all reason, should have been replaced by the ologies and isms of modern times, but which in spite of all human estimation has persisted and influenced and comforted and fed and cured and sheltered and championed and reconciled. That is a miracle at least on par with walking on water! Yet we doubt, we put off, sometimes we debate without purpose, we speculate a hundred reasons why we shouldn't try the untried, supposing that the mood is not right or the economy is not auspicious or the church is no longer in the miracle business but should be satisfied simply to survive in a world in which the wind may come up at any moment.

But just look at the great miracle presented in this congregation today—wealthy and modest, infant and aged, broker and mechanic, Pakistani and Hispanic and African-American and Anglo, having nothing in common but the most vital thing of all, which the world does not esteem and hardly credits but without which we confess that there is no life—our faith in God as God has manifested himself in Jesus Christ! And it has been so with this congregation, now to a greater degree, now to a lesser degree, but nevertheless always to a *miraculous* degree, for one hundred fifteen years, and so it has been with our denomination for two hundred four years, and so it has been with the

Nineteenth Sunday in Ordinary Time

Reformed family for over four hundred years, and so it has been with the Christian church for almost two thousand years. That is how long people have been walking on water at the bidding of Jesus Christ. Now how can any of us feel seriously threatened when there arises a wind of doctrinal debate or General Assembly action or inaction or rising costs and falling interest rates? Surely we declare our faith every time we take the risk of working miracles as Christ directed his followers to do—miracles of proclaiming the gospel in imaginative and innovative ways, miracles of raising the outcast to dignity and miracles of seeing that no one in this community, resident or visitor, is hungry, miracles of housing the homeless and miracles of bringing to an end oppression wherever it exists, miracles of curing cancer and heart disease and arthritis and AIDS, miracles of opening closed minds and warming cold hearts and relaxing clenched fists so that the story of the gospel is good news for *everyone*.

We must not be satisfied with only a half-faith! The same Jesus who calls us to faith for *salvation* calls us also to faith for *ministry*. And no one who believes in Jesus will be put to shame. We are the body of Christ—what a miracle of God's safekeeping that the church does not simply exist, but can worship openly, can teach freely, can have fellowship without restraint in most of the world! Jesus Christ calls us bravely and confidently to work miracles in his name. Shall it be bringing Habitat for Humanity to Dodge City? Shall it be providing after-school care for neighborhood children? Shall it be outreach to our growing Hispanic population? The Lord who calls us out of the boat is trustworthy and true. See, we are already walking on water! Why should we fear the wind?

Twentieth Sunday in Ordinary Time
First Presbyterian Church, Dodge City, Kansas
August 15, 1993

Genesis 45:1–15
Romans 11:1–2a, 29–32
Matthew 15:10–28

"God's Way with Evil"

It was just a little before noon in early December, during a break between terms in law school, that my mother and I were traveling south along Highway 17 in North Carolina. I was driving my father's car. We were going to meet my father at the airport in Charleston, South Carolina, and continue on to Florida and a first-time visit to the Virgin Islands. My father had left us at Charlotte to fly up to Philadelphia on business, and my mother and I had spent two or three days visiting friends and historic sites in North Carolina, and we were looking forward to renewing our Southeastern adventure as a family. We had only a couple of hours before my father's flight was scheduled to arrive, but time enough for lunch in the next town with a fast-food restaurant.

But as we drove south along the narrow two-lane highway, a car came around the bend in the opposite direction a quarter of a mile ahead of us, and as it approached us far in excess of the speed limit, it swerved into our southbound lane, then back into its northbound lane and then, just as we were about to pass it, back into our lane. The impact rocked our car; there was damage to the driver's door and the left rear door, and the left rear fender was crunched up to and around the left rear tire. But before we had an opportunity even to stop or think about the damage to our car and the thin margin by which we had escaped injury, I saw in the rear-view mirror the car which had hit us—an old Ford Mustang—collide head-on with the car behind us, and then cartwheel several times with doors and bumpers and gas tank flying into the air as it went. No sooner had we stopped our car and I had gotten out, than two dozen people had appeared, as it seemed, out of nowhere, looking at the remains of the Mustang and the body of its driver sprawled on the shoulder of the highway. The man was dead; I suppose that his neck was broken on impact. A young woman in blue jeans picked up his wallet and found his driver's license. Did anyone know James Macmillan? she asked. People shook their heads, but after the state patrol officer arrived, we were informed that James Macmillan had been arrested for driving while intoxicated the previous night, and had been released from jail just three hours before the accident. Presumably, he had spent a good portion of those three hours drinking again. While most people were gathered around the dead man, some had congregated around the driver of the car which had been directly behind us, the front of which now looked like an accordion. Was he OK? they asked. Yes, he thought so. He had no scrapes or bruises or broken bones, but the young black soldier from Camp Lejeune was blanched like a sheet. He stood up, but after a few seconds, his legs gave way beneath him. Remembering my Boy Scout training about recognizing and treating possible shock, I suggested that he lie down in the back seat of his car, and found a coat to put over him. Eventually, after the patrolman arrived, the man agreed to ride in an ambulance to hospital in Wilmington for an examination.

We told our story to the patrolman and, at his request, I took some photographs with my camera, agreeing to send them to his office when they were developed. Then my mother and I went on our way to the nearest garage to have the fender pulled away from the tire, and from there on to the Charleston airport, where my father would be waiting and wondering whether we had been in some mishap.

For the rest of that trip and for several months afterward, I instinctively pulled over onto the shoulder of the highway whenever an on-coming car gave the slightest hint of crowding or crossing the center line. But as my mother and I drove on to Charleston that day, badly shaken, we talked not only about our narrow survival, but also about the miracle of the man in the car behind us, who, because we had been there to take the first impact and reduce the momentum of the Mustang, survived the demolition of his car alive and without apparent injury. It was tragic enough for one person to have died on that road that day, regardless that it was probably his own drinking that had led to his death. At least, by our simple presence at that place at that time, a double

"God's Way with Evil"

tragedy had been prevented. Was it providence? we wondered. We were in no mood for holiday at that point; we met my father at the Charleston airport and explained what had happened and headed immediately back home to Denver. Our vacation was spoiled and the car was badly damaged, but we considered *that* a comparatively *small* price to pay for the safety of the little soldier from Camp Lejeune, to whose family Christmas must have seemed to come a little early that year.

I remembered a Bible story from a childhood Sunday school lesson, about someone severely wronged by the hatred of others, but whose misfortune God was able to put to great and redemptive use. We can never be sure about such things, at least in the sense of proving it to another person's satisfaction, but I still think, almost twenty years later, that the hand of God was somehow in that incident on Highway 17—certainly not causing the wreck (I do not believe in a God of vengeful destruction, but in a God of purposeful creation), certainly not willing the death of the man whose car hit ours (I do not believe that God is the Lord of death, but that God is the Lord of life), but manifestly working some miracle of redemption out of a situation which appeared, to human logic, hopeless. When I first saw the wrecked car behind us, with virtually nothing left in front of the windshield, I assumed that its occupant must surely be dead, and yet the only physical effect was that he was still shaking like a leaf when I put my arms around him to say goodbye before he got in the ambulance. What had caused our fear and disappointment and inconvenience—the crash of another car into ours—I firmly believe God meant for good—the saving of that man's life, in the car behind us.

Many of us have had such reflections on past experience. In the immediate moment of crisis or perplexity or decision-making, we could see no good, and could feel only anguish, but upon reflection we have detected some blessing which otherwise would not have come to pass but for that incident. I do not believe that God the Father of our Lord Jesus Christ intends that anyone should experience suffering or agony or despair, but the scriptures affirm the ability of God to redeem suffering and agony and despair in fulfillment of the great divine purpose. Hope springing from hopelessness: Is that not, in fact, what the resurrection is all about? That nothing, not even the meanest hatred of the human heart and the cruelest injustice of the human mind, can long frustrate God's loving and merciful purpose of eternal life and the triumph of God's goodness over the powers of evil and death? Even the refusal of individuals to receive the good news of the gospel, God can transform into an opportunity for the Spirit to seek out and find *other* people receptive to the gospel and nurturing of it, channels through which the gospel may yet have fruitfulness among those who have been obstinate in their rejection of it.

Twentieth Sunday in Ordinary Time

So Joseph, hated by his brothers for his attitude of superiority and sold by them into slavery in Egypt, discerned the redemptive work of God when they appeared in front of him pleading for food. Through his experience in Egypt, Joseph had matured out of his haughty conceit to become a person genuinely concerned for the welfare of others. He had grown in wisdom and ability to the point that he was Pharaoh's chief minister, daily making judgments that affected the entire kingdom and each of its citizens. And a part of that wisdom was an appreciation for the inevitability of the purpose of God. How remarkable that Joseph refrained from using his authority to punish his brothers for their despicable act of selling their own kinsman into slavery and the cruel hoax of convincing their father that his beloved son was dead! How remarkable that Joseph perceived in his own suffering and agony and despair that God had worked a marvelous advance toward his ultimate purpose of winning and nurturing a people for himself who would be a fermenting agent for the redemption of the whole world! "I am your brother, Joseph," he revealed himself to them,

> whom you sold into Egypt. And now do not be distressed, or angry with yourselves, because you sold me here; for God sent me before you to preserve life. For the famine has been in the land these two years; and there are five more years in which there will be neither plowing nor harvest. God sent me before you to preserve for you a remnant on earth, and to keep alive for you many survivors. So it was not *you* who sent me here, but *God*. (Gen 45:4b–8a, NRSV)

And Joseph promised to provide for his family and all of their household in Egypt.

We must be careful to distinguish God's steadfastness of purpose from any sort of fatalism. The only *inevitable* element of the incident was that God would work some *redemption* through it. The story does not say that God willed the evil in the heart of Joseph's brothers that caused them to do wickedness. They were free agents in the matter, who out of their own jealousy and fear worked a great wrong against Joseph, and, so, against God as well, for anyone who despises or insults or injures another person despises and insults and injures God. The great theological insight of Genesis in telling the story of Joseph is the affirmation that it is in the secular realm of human choice that God accomplishes the work of salvation; God works out the divine purpose in the very circumstances of and through and despite the free choices and movements of his creatures. It had been Joseph's own artless decision, in his adolescence, to flaunt his dream of his superiority over his brothers. It had been his brothers' own base decision to sell Joseph to a passing caravan headed for

"God's Way with Evil"

Egypt and to deceive their father into thinking that Joseph had been eaten by a wild beast. But ultimately, it was *God* who, working *through* their hateful attitudes and destructive actions reeking of death, brought *not* death but *life*— new life to Joseph, now caring and compassionate and wise, and new life to the family of Israel, now welcome to weather the famine in a land of abundance and safety. And we are reminded of the absolute sovereignty of God and the absolute triumph of God's purpose; even in the face of human arrogance and human deceit, God does not forget his eternal promise of salvation. The bleakest horizons we can imagine are not beyond God's power to set aglow with the sunrise of his gracious love. But it may require the darkness of what appears to be a God-forsaken night to evoke our gratitude for the light of God's day.

Many people's highways seem at first to be scattered with wreckage, but on reflection, the wreckage is perceived to have been the opportunity through which God's purpose of redemption was fulfilled—hatred, divorce, loss of a job, illness, sometimes even death. Does God want individuals to be alienated or nations to be at war? Does God want marriages to fail? Does God want people to be unemployed or sick? Does God want life to end in nothingness? Certainly not. But see what saving wonders God is able to work and *has* worked in and through even such desperate circumstances as these—the evils of injury, of tragedy, of destruction, even of crucifixion! God's way with evil is to bring good out of it.

Twenty-first Sunday in Ordinary Time

Spanish Springs Presbyterian Church, Sparks, Nevada

August 24, 2008

Exodus 1:8—2:10
Romans 12:1–8
Matthew 16:13–20

"Human Fear and Divine Promise"

"Now a new king arose over Egypt, who did not know Joseph. He said to his people, 'Look, the Israelite people are more numerous and more powerful than we. Come, let us deal . . . with them'" (Exod 1:8–10a, NRSV). And so some people set fire to three synagogues in Sacramento a few years ago and a man walked into a Jewish Community Center in Los Angeles and started shooting. Closer to home, a Jewish synagogue in Reno was twice vandalized. An ancient irrationality once again made headlines.

Is it far-fetched, do you think, to relate the paranoia of an Egyptian king who ruled more than three thousand years ago to hate crimes committed in modern-day America? Surely fear and its irrational consequences go back many centuries, and anyone who listens to talk radio or surfs the internet or, unfortunately, attends certain churches, knows that racial and ethnic hatred is a powerful force in our society today—not only hatred of Jews, of course, but African Americans, Hispanics, Asians, gays, even particular political parties. Not too long ago, I was stopped at a traffic light in Sparks behind a pickup truck that had a Rush Limbaugh sticker on one side of the bumper and a sticker on the other side that read, "Communists and Democrats are traitors

"Human Fear and Divine Promise"

to America." Since more than half of the registered voters declaring a party affiliation in this country are Democrats, it made me wonder which America it *was* that the bumper sticker was referring to. Maybe it was intended as some kind of joke. It didn't seem any funnier to me, though, than suggesting that Republicans are Nazis. How far are such *words* removed from *deeds* like torturing a young college student, a gay man, and leaving him to die, arms and legs stretched out on a Wyoming fence? How far are such words removed from deeds like dragging another man behind a pickup truck, an African American, over miles of Texas road until his body falls to pieces?

Hatred and the rhetoric of hatred are thriving in America, sometimes spilling over into bombs and bullets and very frequently claiming marching orders from the Bible—hatred based on fear of people whom we have decided are different from us, people whom the paranoid lump together under a single label and paint with the same brush, gullibly turning anecdote into truism and heretically perverting gospel into propaganda. "Come, let us deal shrewdly with them, or they will increase" (Exod 1:10a, NRSV). "Come, let us deal with them before they become more powerful." "Come, let us deal with them before they take over completely."

The king of Egypt oppressed the Israelites with forced labor. "But the more they were oppressed, the more they multiplied and spread, so that the Egyptians came to dread the Israelites" (Exod 1:12, NRSV). So "[t]he king of Egypt said to the Hebrew midwives . . . , 'When you act as midwives to the Hebrew women, and see them on the birthstool, if it is a boy, kill him . . .' But the midwives feared God; they did not do as the king of Egypt commanded them, but they let the boys live. . . . Then Pharaoh commanded all his people, 'Every boy that is born to the Hebrews you shall throw into the Nile'" (Exod 1:15-22, NRSV). And the river that *had* been Egypt's famed ribbon of *life* became Egypt's infamous gutter of *death*, until *one* baby boy, put in the river but in a basket—the Hebrew word for "basket" here is the same word that is translated as "ark" in the story of Noah—was saved through the waters of the Nile and grew up to lead God's people out of slavery to the promised land. And on their way to the promised land, just as they were about to enter it, Moses reminded them of God's command, "You shall . . . love the stranger, for *you* were strangers in the land of Egypt" (Deut 10:19, NRSV). We sure don't hear *that* spoken of on talk radio, do we? Nor of Paul's appeal for tolerance in the church at Rome, where Gentile Christians were discriminating against Christians of Jewish background. When even Christians in the church draw lines of distinction among each other and value some over others and judge those who have different points of view, the one body becomes a war zone and dishonors Christ, the Prince of Peace.

Twenty-first Sunday in Ordinary Time

What is it about so many people that they have to have an enemy—that they have to have someone to hate, someone to blame when things don't go well for them? It is really no coincidence that the rise of racial and ethnic hatred and violence in the 1990s and early 2000s has come in the wake of the end of the Cold War. For more than forty years, politicians and others could lay the blame for everything that was wrong in the world on our great national enemy, and we *believed* it. We could identify it, we could rally against it, we could point to it on a map. And when the great enemy was dismantled and seemed to be made impotent—more by the faithful witness of a *pope*, I think, than by the *military* strategies of presidents and prime ministers—there was a blank spot in a lot of people's picture of the universe. For so long, it had been "us" versus "them." A whole industry grew up with the promise of destroying *them* even *more* devastatingly than they could destroy *us*. Political figures knew they could get a jump in the polls by talking tough against the Soviets, and not just the radical Joe McCarthys, but even moderates. They understood the value of a society having scapegoats. For that matter, so did Adolf Hitler. But there is a long heritage of identifying other races, other nationalities, other religions, as threats to our nation, threats to our jobs, threats to our families. It's certainly more satisfying for people to be able to point to something *external* as the reason that they are down and out, insignificant in the eyes of society and unremarkable even in the eyes of their in-laws, than to have to deal honestly with their own inability to function in society and get along with their employers. So if they don't have the Soviets anymore, who *can* they blame? Who *can* they hate? Who *is* the cause of everything that is wrong with the world? A long time ago, Pharaoh found the answer, and the Bible tells about it frankly in terms of economic power and ethnic prejudice.

I ministered for several years in a part of the country that could not bring itself to accept the newest wave of immigrants in our *nation* of immigrants. I remember how so many people said that crime and taxes and even potholes were the fault of "those Mexicans," documented or *un*documented. Of course, "those Mexicans" had only come to the area to take the unpleasant, dangerous, low-wage jobs that Americans refused even to apply for—jobs in the beef packing plants, some of which were owned by the very people long considered pillars of the community. It all seemed to reach a head when it came time to consider a bond issue for building more schools. "Why should *we* build schools for *them*?" was a question frequently heard on the streets. "That will just encourage them to breed, and soon there will be more of *them* than there are of *us*. Doesn't it just gall you that they can walk together down an American street speaking a language that we can't understand? They don't even pay taxes!" And of course, that was not true, because, in fact, they paid a

"Human Fear and Divine Promise"

higher percentage of their income in sales taxes and user fees than practically anyone else. And, in fact, the landlords of the buildings where they lived paid property taxes. And it was curious—amusing, even—that one of the objectors to the idea of a Spanish-language worship service in our church was among the first people in his line of business to hire a Hispanic person for his retail staff to bargain with cash-paying Spanish-speaking customers. If they all were to return to Mexico tomorrow, the economies of several states would totally collapse, and state and local governments would be utterly destitute.

So dependent have we become on such cheap labor, it would be economically insane to put the rhetoric into practice and send them or scare them back to Mexico—just as insane as it was when Pharaoh decided to kill off the next generation of the cheap labor that was tilling Egypt's fields and building Egypt's monuments. "Come," said Pharaoh, "let us deal shrewdly with them, or they will increase" (Exod 1:10a, NRSV). "Let us make their lives miserable." In fact, it may be that Pharaoh didn't want the Israelites to multiply because they *might* overthrow their taskmasters and then *leave* the country altogether, and, so, *wreck* the economy. But the more they were *oppressed* (the more harshly the tactics of death were applied to them) the more they multiplied and spread (the more the power of life coursed within them), so that the Egyptians came to *dread* the Israelites. Desperate, Pharaoh next turned to the midwives and ordered them, "When you act as midwives to the Hebrew women, and see them on the birthstool, if it is a boy, kill him" (Exod 1:16a, NRSV). What more horrific parallel to the fear and hatred represented by that decree than bursting into a Jewish children's day camp and firing bullets, as a man did in California a few years ago? And hatred being something that feeds on itself, for good measure, then, gunning down a Filipino letter carrier on the way out of town? "A wake-up call to America," the gunman called it, "to kill the Jews."

It's interesting that, halfway through this passage from the book of Exodus, Pharaoh stops talking about the "Israelites" and starts talking about the "Hebrews." The "Israelites" were literally the descendants of Jacob, who had been invited to live in Egypt by the Pharaoh who so appreciated Joseph's discernment and counsel during the years of drought and famine. But the word "Hebrew" was used in the ancient Near East to mean anyone who was part of a marginal group, someone without social standing, a person who belonged to a class that was sometimes feared, sometimes excluded, sometimes despised—in general, the "have-nots" of society. In his paranoia, Pharaoh was casting a very broad net indeed, like Herod did hundreds of years later. Ironically, the one Jewish child that Pharaoh had *most* to fear is the one who was *saved* from destruction by Pharaoh's own *daughter*, the princess, and came to be *raised* in Pharaoh's own *household*—Moses, who grew up to lead the oppressed

Israelites out of Egypt through the parted waters and then sent them crashing back upon the Egyptian soldiers in pursuit. Ironically, the one Jewish child that *King Herod* had most to fear is the one who was saved from destruction by the counsel of wise men that Mary and Joseph should take him and flee to Egypt until Herod was dead and his decrees with him. And that one became the Messiah, God's own anointed King above all kings. So does God deal in scripture with those quaking little tyrants whose policies of *fear* become habits of *hatred* that fuel deeds of *death*.

When we confess our sin publicly on Sunday mornings, we are confessing not just our personal wrongdoings, but the sinful web of which we are a part. We confess the sin of all of fallen humanity, for we *are* our brothers' and sisters' keepers. To one degree or another, directly or indirectly, we *do* participate in each other's sin. It may be by laughing at or not objecting to a joke that ridicules a person or a race or a religion or a nationality or a disability. It may be by using terminology that demeans another because of skin color or language or food preference. It may be by jumping to conclusions about a whole group of people based on the offensive behavior of some. It may be by saying, "It's none of my business," or "The problem is so big that I can't make a difference, so I won't even try." It may be our willingness to swallow an absurdity, or to live in the world as if God's love for *all* of humankind attested in scripture were not a judgment upon every hateful thought and every careless word and every faithless deed. We, each of us, need to be vigilant against speech that demeans, actions that degrade, attitudes that dehumanize, silence that condones. And we must not give up our personal responsibility within society and within our families, simply because we discover that the answers to hatred and violence are not easy and the results of remedial measures are not quick.

The good news is that human fear cannot defeat God's promise. For all of Pharaoh's cruelty, God's purpose of liberation and redemption, God's future of blessing and destiny, was fulfilled nevertheless. The tactics of destruction and fear only had the effect of preserving and saving. Oppression produced a Moses, God's own instrument in fulfilling God's purpose of life. And every human empire ever since stands judged by how it treats the "Hebrews"—that is, the marginal, the poor, the despised, the stranger. "For," scripture says, "the Lord your God is God of gods and Lord of lords, the great God, mighty and awesome, who is not partial and takes no bribe, who executes justice for the orphan and the widow, and who loves the strangers. . . . *You* shall *also* love the stranger, for *you* were strangers in the land of Egypt" (Deut 10:17–18a, 19, NRSV).

TWENTY-SECOND SUNDAY IN ORDINARY TIME

Spanish Springs Presbyterian Church, Sparks, Nevada

SEPTEMBER 1, 2002

Exodus 3:1–15
Romans 12:9–21
Matthew 16:21–28

"Prescription for an Icy Heart"

In mid-October, about six weeks from now, the Reno area will have its local CROP Walk to combat world hunger. Promoted in communities all across the country by Church World Service, CROP walkers are volunteers who are sponsored by people donating, on a pledge basis, so many cents or dollars per mile walked on a prescribed route of five miles or so. I hope to have information available for you about the CROP Walk leading up to the event; I've participated in the organization of CROP Walks and have walked in them myself in Texas and Nebraska and Kansas.

When I was in Dodge City, the regional director for Church World Service came to town to visit with the local CROP Walk organizers. She commented that one particular poster that had been printed to publicize the CROP Walk was being discontinued because so many people had said that they did not care for it. The poster, which I already had up on display in our church building, showed a child lying on a sidewalk in some back-alley of a city. The caption below the picture read: "Jesus Christ slept here." The Church World Service representative said that she did not understand why so many churches and local CROP Walk committees disliked the poster. But several of us present at the meeting voiced the opinion that the poster was probably unpopular because it was so graphically true; Jesus identified with those who are little cared *for* and little cared *about* in this world, the lowly and the despised.

Jesus himself was frequently treated like a homeless person, an alien, a refugee, someone to be ignored or to be silenced. We must remember that the cross, which we proclaim in *song* as something *wondrous*, something in which we *glory*, is *first* of all a thing of *shame*. It was the Roman instrument of torture for thieves and for revolutionists—those who robbed the rich and those who plotted to overturn the prevailing order. Jesus disappointed some by refusing to take up the sword or to assume the title of king, but his affections and his attentions and his assertions made him enemies among people of pride and power and privilege. So, ultimately, he was crucified. When Jesus told the disciples that anyone who wished to be his follower must take up a cross and follow him, he was telling them that they and all future disciples must be willing to be ridiculed and scorned, and to suffer humiliation and disgrace. "God forbid it, Lord!" Peter objected when Jesus spoke of what would happen to him in Jerusalem. "This must *never* happen to *you*" (Matt 16:22b, NRSV). Peter might well have added, "Because I never want it to happen to *me*." "But [Jesus] turned and said to Peter, 'Get behind me, Satan! You are a stumbling block to me; for you are setting your mind not on divine things but on human things. . . . [T]hose who want to save their life will lose it, and those who lose their life for my sake will find it'" (Matt 16:23, 25, NRSV).

In our praise of Jesus Christ, we use words like "glorious" and "great" and "triumphant." But Jesus himself seems to have understood glory and greatness and triumph as having to do with forbearance and humility and rejection. He did not expect to have his way by right. He did not demand preeminence over others as the representative of God. He did not insist even upon the courtesy of being listened to. He refused to take it upon himself to impose a political agenda, as if by divine prerogative. There is no suggestion in the scriptures that Jesus had a winning personality in the ordinary sense of "charm" or that he possessed a commanding physical appearance. Indeed, the Bible implies that Jesus would have been a poor advertisement for Dale Carnegie, and all the artists who have rendered Jesus as a ruggedly handsome, athletic hero have done a disservice to generations of Christians by disfiguring the message of the Gospel writers. *They* proclaim that Jesus is the fulfillment of Isaiah's testimony about the suffering servant despised and rejected, without form or comeliness, wounded, bruised, oppressed, and afflicted. Probably all of us are at least mildly offended to think that Jesus might just be more at home sleeping on the streets alongside the child in rags than pampered in our freshly made up, clean-linened guest room, where his presence under our roof would

"Prescription for an Icy Heart"

make us the envy of our friends. "If any want to become my followers, let them deny themselves and take up their cross and follow me" (Matt 16:24, NRSV), says Jesus to would-be disciples today—not merely skipping dessert during Lent, not just enduring the minor inconveniences and major disappointments that are a normal if unhappy part of life, and not proudly strutting down a boulevard lined with applauding admirers.

Generally speaking, the Old Testament and other Jewish writings did not expect a *suffering* Messiah. They expected a Messiah who would *inflict suffering* on the *enemies* of Israel and would punish the wicked *within* Israel. Indeed, the first disciples, so far from regarding the crucifixion as a sign of Jesus' Lordship, scattered into hiding the moment he was arrested, most of them. In spite of Jesus' several predictions of his passion, Peter and the rest seem to have been totally unprepared for what actually happened in Jerusalem that Good Friday. Nearly two thousand years later, people are *still* unprepared for the cross. Even many of us who proudly identify ourselves as Christians are uncomfortable and scandalized by everything that the cross represents.

So, too, many of us who are accustomed to cheering on Paul as he preaches of sin and judgment, and who congratulate ourselves for escaping his lists of wrongdoing (or at least for being able to offer reasonable explanation if we happen to be included in them), find ourselves coming to an abrupt halt when we read the fourteenth verse of the twelfth chapter of Romans: "Bless those who persecute you; bless and do not curse them" (Rom 12:14, NRSV). Paul writes that we are not to repay evil for evil, as if we had the right to avenge God by retaliating against whoever has insulted us, his obviously faithful servants. The apostle recognized the human tendency to identify as *God's* enemies those people who displease *us* in some way. We think that God wants what *we* want. Petty disagreements, especially in the church, quickly escalate into holy wars. But such things can happen only if we have forgotten the humility of Christ, the forbearance of Christ, the patience of Christ, and so allow ourselves to be conquered by the arrogant and proud and vengeful spirit of the world.

If we have permitted the world to bend us to its own way, we are no longer in the way of the *cross*. For the world is not interested in living in harmony. The world encourages us to be haughty. The world ridicules those who associate with the lowly. The world seduces us into claiming to be wiser than we are. See how far all of this is from the example of Jesus Christ! Ought we to be silent in the face of evil? Ought we to stand aside while oppressors work injustice and woe? Ought we to say to the hungry and the homeless and the abused, "God will take care of you," and turn away? No. We are to give witness to Jesus Christ in all things. We have a duty to speak out against evil. We have an obligation to work for dignity and peace and justice. We have a responsibility to feed and shelter and defend the poor and the powerless. And that will surely make *us* enemies, as it made *Jesus* enemies. And that may well make *us* unpopular, as it made the *prophets* unpopular. And that will perhaps even make *us* targets of persecution, as it made the *early* Christians targets of persecution. And the instinctive thing to do will be to lash out at cold-hearted people who criticize us, who slander us, who abuse us for simply trying to follow Jesus Christ by helping the alien and confronting the insensitive and renouncing vain self-indulgence for a life of generous servanthood. But to confess Jesus Christ truly means to walk the way of the cross in one's daily life, and that requires living peaceably with all people and doing good to all people. If your enemies are hungry, Paul reminds us, do not avenge yourself by *withholding* your *generosity* from them; *feed* them. If your enemies are thirsty, Paul instructs us, do not stoop to worldly pride by *refusing* them *compassion*; give them something to *drink*. The same is as true of *nations* as of *individuals*.

And then Paul quotes a line from Proverbs which is very interesting and easily misunderstood: "[F]or by doing this you will heap burning coals on their heads" (Rom 12:20b, NRSV). At first blush, that contradicts all of Paul's teaching about not seeking revenge, not usurping the judgment of God, by the image of burning coals, hot, searing, excruciatingly painful, piled upon the head of anyone to whom we return good for evil. If it is Christ-like to be gracious toward our enemies, then surely it is *un*-Christ-like in the extreme to plot our revenge indirectly, flashing our enemies an insincere smile behind which lies the satisfaction of knowing that God is going to punish them for being such rotten people.

In fact, people in Paul's time would not have associated burning coals with meting out punishment and destruction so much as with the process of refining and cleansing. It is the heritage of medieval morality plays that causes us to assume that by talking about heaping burning coals on people's heads, Paul is promising a finer revenge than we ourselves could ever work. No, what Paul is talking about is the hope that, as a result of our patient forbearance which steadfastly *refuses* to return evil for evil, the *enemy*—the one who has abused us, who has ridiculed us, who has slandered us, who has injured us—will eventually turn away from his or her enmity and will become a friend. Our gracious and humble and loving deeds toward those who do us wrong are God's prescription for that person's icy heart which will melt it, which will soften it, which will warm it, which will burn away the hatred which is a canker within it. Vengeance is *God's* concern, not *ours*; there is no place in the Christian life for the pride and jealousy and self-centeredness out of which thoughts of revenge spring. Our own suffering must never become an excuse for wishing *another's* suffering. The standard by which the *Christian* deals with

"Prescription for an Icy Heart"

others must always be reconciliation and peace. For that is how *God* dealt with *us* when we were *his* enemies, and that is how God has determined to deal *through us* with those who continue to oppose the divine will.

Jesus Christ deserved a palace, but he was well content to sleep on the hard pavement. Jesus Christ deserved a throne of glory, but he was fully willing to take his place on a cross of shame. And that cross continues to be the most potent instrument for thawing icy hearts. It really is not enough for the Christian to confess Jesus as Messiah and Lord. The Christian must be willing to acknowledge Jesus as the *suffering* Messiah and the *crucified* Lord, and not only to proclaim that conviction in *words*, but to *practice* it daily in her or his own life. Only by our doing so, wishing our enemy good and not ill, offering ourselves in humble service and not claiming for ourselves a place of privilege, can we participate in God's great purpose of redemption, Christ's glorious ministry of reconciliation, the Holy Spirit's triumph over cold, hard hearts. Only by our doing so, adopting the ways of Jesus as our pattern for living, accepting even the possibility of our own discomfort and rejection, does the cross become a sign of salvation. Only by our doing so, bearing the truth of God's merciful love on *our* shoulders and surrendering *ourselves* totally to God's will for the good of all creation, do we become genuine followers of Jesus Christ.

Twenty-third Sunday in Ordinary Time
Spanish Springs Presbyterian Church, Sparks, Nevada
September 4, 2005

Exodus 12:1–14
Romans 13:8–14
Matthew 18:15–20

"Not for Empire"

In its sixtieth year, the United Nations finds itself under a lot of criticism in this country. Founded in response to the wreckage of war, the purpose of the United Nations was to find peaceful *alternatives* to war as a means of settling disputes between countries. A lot of Americans, and of course the administration, were angry and eventually dismissive of the United Nations when it refused to bless the war in Iraq. Others have recently pointed to instances of corruption and have charged excessive bureaucracy as indications of the urgent need of reform. But long before any of *these* things, *some* people in the United States opposed simply the *idea* of a United Nations, arguing that the United States should never give up an inch of its sovereignty, never an iota of decision-making, and certainly nothing like a veto, to any other nation or group of nations. They chafe at the phrase "one world," and vow to oppose anything that smacks of a global governing body.

Over the past couple of decades, though, we have witnessed, with hardly any criticism at all, the rise of supernational *corporations* which wield *enormous* power in the daily lives of people, structured often to escape effective regulatory control by *any* government, undermining not only the *economic*

"Not for Empire"

sovereignty of nations, but the *cultural* heritage of lands and peoples, dictating policy and pouring millions of dollars into national political campaigns. The popular term for it is "globalization," a word that has a nice ring to it, but one that has come to stand for the transfer of American jobs to low-wage, no-benefits, high-pollution countries, all in the name of a goal that sounds very laudable—"free markets." But a lot of people in the world don't wish to have unregulated capitalism imposed upon them, nor local independent businesses destroyed by a handful of "big-box" retailers, nor diets dictated by fast-food mega-chains, nor health ruined by tobacco companies' aggressive marketing even to *children* in *their* countries what they have been forced to admit in the *United States* are products that cause cancer and heart disease. Throughout history, kings and generals have dreamed of empires, and some have achieved them, at least for a while, conquering first this neighbor and then that. But in an era in which stock price and market share are *every*thing and in which war is no longer considered a *glorious* thing, we are discovering that a nation need never fire a single rifle in order to create an empire.

Historians will one day decide whether "globalization" was a good idea. In the short run, however, anything that leads a people to sense that they have lost control over their lives, control over their communities, control over their destiny, will raise up and popularize more and more Osama bin Ladens, and make them *somebody's* heroes. Without in the least bit excusing what Al Qaeda did and does, we had better start acknowledging that such an organization would not exist if people in the Middle East did not perceive a threat to their culture—their religion, their economy, their very identity.

The Bible sanctions no one form of government; there was no such thing as a real democracy in biblical times, and the closest thing to it—Greece—proved to be an *enemy* of God's chosen people, against whom great heroes of the faith revolted. God did indeed raise up *kings* for Israel and Judah, but only because the people grumbled that *other* nations had kings and *they didn't*, and *despite* God's warning that they were better off *without* kings. The Bible voices no preference for one economic theory over another; there was no such thing as free market capitalism in biblical times, and the closest the Bible comes to commending anything that we have witnessed in our own day is the commune—communalism—in which everything within a community is voluntarily shared and distributed according to need. But the notion that the *government* is owed unquestioning allegiance, personified in its ruler, or that the *economy* is of prime importance, in the way of efficiency of production and the creation of scads of wealth, or that human well-being is assured by any scheme or goal of *human* making, is debunked from the beginning of the book to the end. The world was created by *God's* hands and is to be used for

Twenty-third Sunday in Ordinary Time

God's purpose, Genesis declares, and the new Jerusalem that is promised in Revelation will descend from *heaven*, not be raised up by Donald Trump or Steve Wynn. The goals of wealth and power and prestige are judged unworthy by the prophets and by Christ himself, and scripture declares that God will reverse for all eternity the fortunes that have prevailed in the few short years of our earthly life. And those who raise up monuments to themselves, those who govern not for the sake of being a blessing to the poor but for the purpose of aggrandizing themselves and their friends, those who rule *not* in humble reliance upon *God* but in defiance of God's redemptive purpose for all of creation even as they make a grand show of their religious piety, *these* people, the Bible declares, will eventually be brought *low* and their empires shall *crumble*. Many a king of Israel, many a king of Judah, failed to heed the lesson of the Israelites' own liberation from slavery in Egypt.

There was no ruler in the world so powerful as Pharaoh. And there was no economy so massive as Egypt's. And there was no army so intimidating as the one that guarded its borders and asserted its will. And there was no society so well-organized to *perpetuate* its power and its prosperity and its might. Who wouldn't want what Egypt had? Who wouldn't envy it, desire it, submit to it? But there were *some*, and, by any *earthly* estimation, they were the least likely to succeed in challenging the "system." Pharaohs thought they had neutralized their threat to the way things were by making slaves of them, even—and this was a great humiliation, really—putting them to work building the pyramids by which the pharaohs proclaimed themselves to be gods.

But it was the *slaves* who had the ear of the one and only *true* God. God was on the side of the poor and the oppressed, not the abusive and the dictatorial. God heard their cries of suffering and hardship, and God determined to bring them out of slavery into the place that God had promised their ancestors, where they could be free to worship and free to grow into the sort of society that would demonstrate God's will for all people, whose very existence would be a judgment upon greed and injustice and wickedness and impiety and fear and death—the very things that characterize an empire. Pharaoh had made the foreigners a scapegoat for all that was wrong or that might *go* wrong in his society; in the eyes of the Egyptians, they deserved nothing *better* than to be slaves. But God would make of these slaves a light to the nations, a blessing to the Gentiles, a seed that would sprout and grow and bear fruit for the benefit of all. First, though, they had to escape the clutches of empire; all that the empire offered as enticement, all that the empire strived for as goal, all that the empire called good, they must renounce, expose for what it really was, turn away from, and resolve never to imitate. God was about to work a mighty act of liberation. They must forever remember what it was like to live under

"Not for Empire"

Pharaoh's heel, and never again submit to it, or subject others to it, but devote all *their* energies to building a just and equitable society that *truly* glorified God.

And so, on the eve of their liberation, they were to eat and dress not as people who were at home in the empire, but as people who were intent on journeying away from it, restless under a regime erected on greed and fear, indignity and impoverishment, and bound instead for a promised land of justice and prosperity, not just for some but for all, not dependent on the tactics of oppression but on the promise of freedom, not based on the competition of scarcity but on the sharing of abundance, not for the glory of a king but for the glory of God. They were to prepare and eat a special meal in a special way, as if outdoors, not kenneled in the cage of Pharaoh's threats and falsehoods but poised for the long and difficult journey to freedom from everything that stifled the fullness of God's promise.

> This is how you shall eat it: your loins girded, your sandals on your feet, and your staff in your hand; and you shall eat it hurriedly. It is the passover of the Lord. For I will pass through the land of Egypt that night, and I will strike down every firstborn in the land of Egypt, both human beings and animals; on all the gods of Egypt I will execute judgments: I am the Lord. . . . This day shall be a day of remembrance for you. You shall celebrate it as a festival to the Lord; throughout your generations you shall observe it as a perpetual ordinance. (Exod 12:11–12, 14, NRSV)

The community of faith was annually ever after to celebrate this festival of urgent departure. To fail to remember and recount and repeat the story by reenacting the meal would run the risk of feeling at home in some empire, comfortable with the empire's values, mimicking the empire's ways, and *this*, God's people must never do. They must never submit again to slavery of any kind. And they must never forget what it was like to be the victims of empire, so that they would never be tempted to create an empire that would victimize *others*. It was not for *empire* that God chose a people to be his own—neither to suffer under empire nor adopt *themselves* the ways of empire. *Their* authority was not *Pharaoh* but *God*. *Their* truth was not *Pharaoh's* decrees but *God's*. *Their* destiny was not the *allurements* of the *bazaar* but the *joy* of *salvation*. *Their* methods were not to be *fear* and *threat* and *coercion*, but *love* and *mercy* and *peace*. *Their* trust was not to be in *weapons* and *soldiers* and *possessions* and *accounts*, but in the faithful promises of *God*.

The ways of empire have an attraction, surely. To be a slave is at least to have assurance of your next meal, even if it is unappetizing. To be a slave is not to have to take any responsibility for the way things are, and therefore a

Twenty-third Sunday in Ordinary Time

slave cannot be held *accountable* for the way things are. To be a slave is not to have to exercise any independent moral judgment—you just do what you are told. But to be a slave is not to be fully human, not to be what God created us to be. God created us to have and exercise freedom, which means to live with the risk of hunger, to be accountable for our behavior and for the welfare of the communities to which we belong, and to be moral beings.

After they finally escaped from Egypt through the parted waters of the Red Sea, there would be times in the wilderness when the Israelites would long for the assurances and certainties of life under the empire and a slave's exemption from moral responsibility. It was easier to bow down to Pharaoh, who threatened death, and pray to his idols made by human hands, than to worship the God who cannot be seen but who is the genuine giver of life. And it was easier to perform the role assigned by the empire, to be simply a cog in Egypt's system of production and consumption, than to face and resist ungodly temptations, having to discern for oneself what was right and good not on the basis of what would profit *Pharaoh* but on the basis of what would please *God*. To live in the empire was, ultimately, to do whatever would fill one's belly. To live in freedom was, daily, to raise the dignity of the spirit above the cravings of the flesh. To live in the empire was to scramble for oneself, to claw one's way to the top. To live in freedom was to count one's neighbor just as worthy of respect and well-being as oneself. Many years later, Jesus would teach his disciples to subvert the mentality of empire in the most radical way: "[L]ove your neighbor as yourself" (Matt 19:19b, NRSV). Not only would *obeying* that command fulfill all of the *other* commandments of God. It would, and it has, toppled tyrants and despots, and has dissolved the fear and greed and pride and lust and self-centeredness that creates empires to begin with and then feeds them and enables them to grow.

The heyday of Egypt is long past, and that of Babylon and Greece and Rome. The Spanish empire is over, and the French and the British. The Nazi empire belongs ignominiously to history, and the Japanese and the Soviet. But the sort of thinking that creates and sustains empires is still with us, perhaps more subtle now than in times past, less dependent upon guns, but just as dangerous to freedom, including the spiritual freedom that is God's intention and Paul's heritage and Jesus' gift through his death on the cross. Consumerism, materialism, convenience, ease—whoever promises and delivers gratification of the flesh today is our society's new Pharaoh, and we are susceptible of being quickly enthralled to them and lulled into disregard for our neighbor in Latin America, in Asia, in Africa, the person down the street whose pension is taken away with the stroke of a pen or whose job is sent to Indonesia with a shrug of shoulders. "For freedom Christ has set us free," Paul wrote to the Galatians.

"Not for Empire"

"Stand firm, therefore, and do not submit again to a yoke of slavery" (Gal 5:1, NRSV)—physical *or* spiritual; the one inevitably will involve the other. Nor, Paul would surely add, be a participant in imposing a yoke of slavery on others. For love does no wrong to a neighbor. Remember your spiritual ancestors who were enslaved in Egypt, and how they were instructed to eat the meal of liberation from slavery, the meal of hasty departure from empire—loins girded, sandals on the feet, staff in hand, hurriedly, for the *empire* was not their home and *slavery* was not their destiny, *nor* should it be *anybody's*.

Twenty-fourth Sunday in Ordinary Time

Spanish Springs Presbyterian Church, Sparks, Nevada

September 11, 2011

Exodus 14:19–31
Romans 14:5–12
Matthew 18:21–35

"The Hardest Thing"

Our society has become obsessed with voicing opinion about what is right and what is wrong, and with finding fault and assessing blame. I suppose that is part of the appeal of the current rash of daytime television talk shows that strive to outdo each other with examples of immodest and outrageous conduct and foul and vituperative language, and all the "Judge So-and-So" programs that feed an insatiable appetite for hearing about people behaving badly and cashing in on it, so to speak, by getting a few moments of fame or notoriety, risking all decency and dignity to see their faces on the screen. It wouldn't be happening, of course, if there weren't a ready audience. The growing and appalling phenomenon of regarding other people's scandal as one's own entertainment seems to condone our rendering judgment upon others and their lives. In the end, of course, it matters not a bit what *we* may think about the situation, but somehow viewers must feel better for having been invited to form their *own* opinions and impose their *own* verdicts on people they will never meet and events they will probably never experience. And they call it "reality TV."

"The Hardest Thing"

But popular opinion seems to be often questionable. We are too quick to view the world and others through the lens of our personal interests and appetites and prejudices. And no single individual ever has all of the "facts," and two people can seldom agree on exactly which facts are relevant, and people often cannot agree on whether something is a *fact* or *not*. Even when we appeal to history books to discover the "truth" about some event that occurred in the past, we often find conflicting accounts, different opinions, of why something happened and the "rightness" or "wrongness" of it. Stalin and Hitler have their defenders. Torture has its defenders. Colonialism has its defenders. There are people out there who even defend *slavery*, at least in specific historic instances. And this is among civilized, polite, educated society. Germany, in the first decades of the twentieth century, was one of the most highly-educated and highly-cultured nations in Europe. Most of us would regard England, upon whose empire of colonies the sun never set, as the epitome of civilization. The American South was known for its gentility and graciousness, and the American North, which long benefited in its own way from the Southern slave economy, was known for its economic enterprise and industrial genius. Eli Whitney, whose cotton gin relied on slave labor, was born in Massachusetts and died in Connecticut.

The Bible, of course, is frequently appealed to as the ultimate standard of right and wrong. It's where we find the Ten Commandments. It's where we find the Sermon on the Mount. And it's where we find instances of divine judgment on all sorts of activity. There is something appealing about the neatness with which it enumerates rules, pronounces statutes, spells out regulations. But then the neatness seems to get a little fuzzy when we read further, beyond the codes and the lists and the tables, particularly when we get into the New Testament. In fact, to some people over the centuries, it has almost seemed like we are dealing with two different Gods in the Bible, two different sets of demands. And when we come to passages such as today's readings from Romans and from Matthew, perhaps our confidence in the ability to render judgments about people and events begins to get precarious altogether.

"Welcome those who are weak in faith, but not for the purpose of quarreling over opinions. Some believe in eating anything, while the weak eat only vegetables" (Rom 14:1–2, NRSV). What's the point of all those rules about food in the Old Testament, then, about not eating certain kinds of meat and about not eating food that has been offered to idols? One of those rules, or both, had apparently prompted a quarrel between Christians in the church at Rome. Some of them maintained that their freedom in Christ had set them at liberty to disregard the old prohibitions on pork and shellfish and the like, and that, since Christians know that idols are not really gods at all, the food that had been offered at pagan *shrines* was perfectly acceptable on Christian *dinner tables*. Others were absolutely appalled at such disregard of the law. "Some judge one day to be better than another, while others judge all days to be alike" (Rom 14:5a, NRSV). Were specific days *required* to be fast days? Could certain things *not* be done on the sabbath? Was *that* what some of the quarreling was about? Well, surely the apostle Paul could set them straight, could let them know what was right and what was wrong.

But if we want Paul to render a decision that we can apply in our own disagreements, we will be disappointed. "Those who eat must not despise those who abstain, and those who abstain must not pass judgment on those who eat; for God has welcomed them" (Rom 14:3, NRSV). What kind of limp answer is that? "Let all be fully convinced in their own minds" (Rom 14:5b, NRSV). What? Is he saying it's just up to each one of us to follow our own conscience, no matter how well or poorly developed? "Who are you to pass judgment on servants of another? It is before their own lord that they stand or fall. . . . Why do you pass judgment on your brother or sister? Or you, why do you despise your brother or sister? For we will all stand before the judgment seat of God" (Rom 14:4a, 10, NRSV). So are we just to let everyone do his or her own thing, regardless of consequences? And then there's Jesus' parable about the servant who owed an astronomical amount of money to his king, most likely the result of gross mismanagement or embezzlement on a grand scale that could never be repaid, but who was forgiven his wrongdoing, but then would *not* forgive the debt that was owed to *him* that, while sizeable, was *nothing* compared to his *own* malfeasance.

What's the point of having rules, statutes, regulations, if, in the end, it doesn't matter whether one does right or one does wrong, or if a person can't even say with certainty that there *is* a right or wrong? What are Paul and Jesus playing at here? Is everyone allowed to do whatever he or she wants in this life, no matter how monstrous, how heinous, how deadly, simply on the promise or hope that punishment will be rendered in some afterlife? Or is it, perhaps, that the issue of right and wrong, in *God's* assessment, has as much to do with *our response* to another's words and deeds as it has to do with what *that* person *said* or *did*? We are *not* ultimately responsible for the attitudes and actions of *others*, even though we may have helped shape and prompt them, directly or indirectly, intentionally or inadvertently. But we *are* ultimately responsible for our *own*, including feelings of vengeance and actions of revenge. And we are responsible for overstepping the bounds of our servant status and creatureliness, presuming to make decisions and take actions that are really only the prerogative of the Master, presuming to know the mind of the Creator so perfectly that we can act in the Creator's stead. Both Jesus and Paul taught

"The Hardest Thing"

that one should first put under the moral microscope one's *own* attitudes and behavior. When one does so, he or she will be loathe to condemn others. And when one considers one's own responsibility for injuring *others*, sometimes inflicting deep pain and suffering not directly, perhaps, but even by one's silence, then the gracious and generous forgiveness of God *must* prompt gracious and generous forgiveness of *others*. It is a tenet of the Christian faith that each of us had a hand in the crucifixion of Jesus, though we were not there, though we were not yet born, because our words and actions today *continue* to reject him, to deny him, to cast judgment upon him, to nail him to the cross. And yet, *we* have been *forgiven*.

Peter thought he was being generous indeed with his suggestion of the number of times he proposed forgiving a brother or a sister. But Jesus countered that Peter was not being generous *enough*. Peter and all of Christ's followers must, in effect, be ready and willing to forgive an *infinite* number of times, and apparently even without repentance on the part of the wrongdoer. From the cross, Jesus prayed for his executioners' pardon, though not a one of them had repented, and *we* are to follow the example of *Jesus*. When Jesus startled Peter with his answer, it was shortly after our Lord had predicted his own death, unjustly, at the hands of others in Jerusalem. Doubtless, Peter's sense of justice, as ours, was offended at the notion that a wrongdoer (and a repeat offender at that!) be forgiven without any show of contrition, or without payment of some earthly penalty. But in *God's* scales of justice, it is just as wrong *not* to forgive the wrongdoer as it was for the wrongdoer to commit the offense in the *first place*. And the Bible offers no limit on the dimensions of the wrong that must be so freely and so completely forgiven.

It may be that the forgiveness itself is a form of judgment, but the psychology and judicial theory of that is not the Christian's first concern. Such forgiveness is itself costly—it *surely* costs us our *pride*, it *may* cost us our *fortune*, it *will* cost us our *indignation*, it *must* cost us our *revenge*. I am sure that, in some places at some times, *preaching* about it has even cost the minister his or her job. But I don't think it's a preacher's responsibility to tell his or her congregation that Jesus didn't really mean what he said.

So how do we keep the world as we know it functioning and still be faithfully obedient to the very rigorous expectations of Jesus Christ our Lord and Master? Or does it perhaps mean that the world in fact would be a very different place? The scriptures teach that Christians must be bold enough in their faith and trusting enough in God to be willing to find out. All the lists of rules, all the codes of statutes, all the books of regulations, boil down to this, Jesus said: "In everything do to others as you would have them do to you; for this is the law and the prophets" (Matt 7:12, NRSV). God will not judge us on the basis of what *others* did to *us*, but on the basis of what *we* did to *others*. And the measure of how much *we* will be *forgiven* is the amount that *we* forgive *others*. So Jesus also said, "Do not judge, so that you may not be judged" (Matt 7:1, NRSV). And it was for teachings like *that* that he was condemned and put to death—the only person who was ever really qualified to *judge* was *himself* judged and condemned to the ultimate punishment by the very ones who were guilty.

Our own refraining from judgment is to begin in the church, where we surely must presume that each person, having confessed the faith and been baptized and endowed with gifts by the Holy Spirit, is acting on the basis of what he or she truly believes to be right, not out of spite or vengeance or self-interest. That doesn't mean that injury or hurt will not occur, and it does not mean that they should not be pointed out. Although we today consider dietary matters to be rather insignificant and wonder how such things could ever be allowed to spiral into dissension and division, we need to recognize that, in the early church, it was a major issue that touched deeply-held convictions about the authority of scripture and obedience to God. But beyond the rightness or wrongness of eating this food or that, or observing this holy day or that, was the question of the rightness or wrongness of judging someone else's actions that represented her or his convictions of faith. The purpose of learning not to judge others *within* the church was so that the same forgiveness would be expressed toward people *outside* the church. And the purpose of learning not to judge others for what some might consider *minor* breaches was so that we would be able to forgive those who commit *great* offenses, even as God has forgiven those who put to death his own Son. That is difficult for individuals. That is difficult for families. It is difficult for faith traditions. It is difficult for nations.

I suppose that, though he created billions of stars in billions of galaxies, and though he raised the mountains and filled the seas, and though he set in motion the forces that organize millions of cells into living, breathing beings, forgiving us for putting to death his Son must be the hardest thing God has ever done. Jesus teaches us that *we* must be willing to do such a hard thing, too.

Twenty-fifth Sunday in Ordinary Time

Spanish Springs Presbyterian Church, Sparks, Nevada

September 21, 2008

Exodus 16:2–15
Philippians 1:21–30
Matthew 20:1–16

"Justice"

If we haven't been offended by some of the sayings of Jesus, we haven't been paying attention. If we haven't been chagrined by many of the deeds of Jesus, we haven't thought much about them. If we have nodded our heads in pious affirmation at everything that Jesus said and did, we haven't been honest with ourselves. For we are not so far removed from the manners and attitudes of people back then, and it was primarily for the *church*, not for people *outside* the church, that the books of the New Testament—the Gospels, Acts, and the epistles—were written, and it was to the people of the church gathered in worship that the books of the New Testament—the Gospels, Acts, and the epistles—were read.

So, when the Gospel writer wrote that Jesus confronted the Pharisees or reproved the scribes or corrected the disciples, the Gospel writer was very likely confronting or reproving or correcting some behavior or attitude that he saw in his own church. And, by extension, the Gospel writer is addressing us today, in the modern church, who often exhibit the same behavior or harbor the same attitude that our spiritual forebears showed or had. As long as we can insulate ourselves from the situation addressed in scripture by thousands of

Twenty-fifth Sunday in Ordinary Time

miles of geography or hundreds of years of history, we can keep up our pious nodding. As long as we can think that the words of scripture are really aimed at people who aren't yet in the church, are still in need of conversion from their sinful ways and have yet to be affiliated with the Christian community, we can avoid making the changes in our own ways of thinking and acting that we are certain are required of those *other* people. But, when we reflect deeply about it, Jesus' way of telling a story has a way of peeling off the layers of foreignness and anonymity, and we find that, through the words of the Gospels, Jesus is confronting *us*, reproving *us*, correcting *us* for behaviors and attitudes, some of which we might even have long assumed were hallmarks of holiness and devotion.

Take, for instance, today's Gospel reading. It is a parable about grace, and we can easily allegorize it to understand that it is making a point about the ability of God to forgive and accept a person late in a sinful life. We might be a little uncomfortable with the notion that somebody who has been a Christian for only a *short* time is just as welcome into heaven as the person who has been a Christian for an entire *lifetime*—that the laborer who worked for only an hour in the vineyard received the same wages as someone who toiled all day long. But, from the standpoint of Christian doctrine, if not always from a conviction of Christian belief, we can affirm that the latecomer is welcome into the Shepherd's flock and fold. More likely, we expect that there will be some special perquisites for the person who has recognized him- or herself as God's sheep all along, has paid up their annual pledge for many years, has been on this committee and that, and has never cheated, gambled, or killed anybody. We might, in fact, wonder whether God's just-ness, so intertwined with God's mercy, is really "justice" at all.

When we speak of "justice" in our society, we usually think of someone winning in a courtroom and someone losing, maybe even being fined, maybe even being imprisoned, maybe even suffering something *worse* in the way of punishment. And young attorneys soon find out that most clients who say they simply seek "justice" really mean that they want a judge or jury to proclaim that they are right and the other party is wrong. In theory, everybody thinks that justice is a fine thing. But usually what we want is justice as *we* define it. We may genuinely desire everyone to experience salvation and eternal life—not just beyond the grave, but here and now. Still, most of us are a little disappointed at the thought that God's gifts of salvation and eternal life are equally for the person who comes to faith later than *we* did.

Jesus, here, was justifying his practice of associating with sinners—in modern parlance, we might say "the unchurched." When he befriended people, it was because they had a need, and he did not discriminate between those

"Justice"

who attended the synagogue or brought sacrifices to the temple and those who did not. The Pharisees had frequently criticized Jesus for such random acts of kindness, though they themselves had rejected what he had to offer. Even his own disciples must have wondered about his lavishing forgiveness and healing and friendship on those whom good Jewish society regarded as unworthy. So Jesus told a story about an employer who was in need of getting his harvest in before it was spoiled. The grapes were at their peak, and a day or two's delay might mean the ruin of the crop. The owner of the vineyard had gone down early in the day and had found some day laborers at the unemployment office. He proposed to pay them what was customary—enough to feed their family for a day—and they had agreed. Apparently, his crop of grapes was so abundant that he soon realized that the original crew could not complete the job before nightfall. He went back to the labor pool mid-morning and was fortunate enough to find some workers who had not yet been engaged for the day. He hired them also, sending them into the field with the promise to pay them whatever was "right"—a rather unspecific arrangement, but one that they jumped at, it seems. He did the same thing at midday and mid-afternoon; apparently, he had woefully underestimated the size of crew that would be needed. Finally, still in need near the end of the day and the situation more urgent because of it, "about five o'clock he went out and found others standing around; and he said to them, 'Why are you standing here idle all day?' They said to him, 'Because no one has hired us.' He said to them, 'You also go into the vineyard'" (Matt 20:6–7, NRSV). So the harvest was saved.

> When evening came, the owner of the vineyard said to his manager, "Call the laborers and give them their pay, beginning with the last and then going to the first." When those hired about five o'clock came, each of them received the usual daily wage. Now when the first came, they thought they would receive more; but each of *them also* received the usual daily wage. And when they received it, they grumbled against the landowner, saying, "These *last* worked only *one hour*, and you have made *them* equal to *us* who have borne the burden of the day and the scorching heat." But he replied to one of them, "Friend, I am doing you no wrong; did you not agree with me for the usual daily wage? Take what belongs to you and go; I choose to give to this last the same as I give to you. Am I not allowed to do what I *choose* with what *belongs* to *me*? Or are you envious because I am generous?" (Matt 20:8–15, NRSV)

Although Jesus spoke it as a parable, we can easily interpret his story about the generous employer as referring to the marvelous generosity of God's grace; even the slowest to respond to God are received with no less enthusiasm than those who have been faithful all their lives. Such is the nature of the kingdom of God. But the story also says something about economics, about how we regard our fellow human beings, about God's concern that everybody receives his or her daily bread. We don't know exactly why there are still some workers available at the unemployment office near the end of the day. One commentator I read jumped to the conclusion that they were too lazy to be there earlier in the day. But the parable itself doesn't support that interpretation. "[A]bout five o'clock [the owner of the vineyard] went out and found others standing around; and he said to them, 'Why are you standing here idle all day?' They said to him, 'Because no one has hired us'" (Matt 20:6–7a, NRSV). The words of the characters in the story—vineyard owner and workers—suggest that they had been there all along, but that there wasn't enough work available for them to be employed. To put it in modern terms, the economy had not generated enough jobs to keep everyone employed. "He said to them, 'You also go into the vineyard'" (Matt 20:7b, NRSV).

When it came time to pay the workers—and the law of Moses requires that every worker is to be paid at the end of each day—the owner of the vineyard, grateful for everyone who had helped bring in the harvest and aware that it took everybody a certain amount of money to put food on the table, paid each worker the same amount, regardless of how many hours he had worked. To have paid those who worked but *one hour* only an eighth or a tenth or a twelfth of what he was paying those who had worked the *entire day* would have left them hungry, and their families, as well. Waiting in the sun is work, too. Anxiously hoping for employment is work, too. At any rate, it seems, as far as God is concerned, equal pay for equal work is not as critical as a living wage for everybody. The issue is equity. Justice, as God understands it, means that everyone is able to eat, that everyone is permitted to live in basic human dignity.

Curiously, the parable specifies that those who were hired last were paid first—itself a situation likely to cause resentment among people inclined to take offense. The workers who had begun harvesting early in the day witnessed the generosity of the owner of the vineyard toward the late-comers, but took it to mean that they surely would receive something extra for laboring so much longer in the hot sun. But they were disappointed when they were given what they had *bargained* for, and nothing more. Had they not performed adequately, that they weren't given a bonus? No—there's no indication that the owner was displeased with their performance. The parable doesn't suggest even that it was the *early* workers' *slowness* that led to the need to hire *additional* laborers to finish the job *on time*. Too bad they couldn't have rejoiced that the families of those hired last would now be fed and at peace!

"Justice"

The righteousness of God sees and rewards the good works that people do. But if we claim God's rewards by *right*, if we compare our *own* performance with that of *others* and judge *them* to be *wanting* instead of giving thanks for the gracious goodness of the Lord before which *all* human accomplishments are *paltry*, aren't we *really* saying that we don't *want* God to be gracious, and aren't we holding the Lord of the universe accountable to selfish human standards of justice?

The parable of Jesus deals with resentment toward others who have actually received the grace that we affirm in theory and sing of in hymns. Grace that can be calculated, grace that is expected, is no longer "grace", and it is certainly not "amazing." It becomes compensation, and something to which we are entitled—something that is ours by right. The Pharisees and many others insisted that reward must be in proportion to performance. That was at the core of their understanding of justice. But Jesus taught that no one is exempt from moral obligation; that being the case, merely being obedient does not entitle *anyone* to special privilege. But, among other things, moral obligation means that we take responsibility for our neighbor having enough to eat, having clothes to wear, having safe shelter, having—all of Jesus' healings on the sabbath shows—access to health care. And the mere fact that no one would hire them for the entire day does not mean that those who worked fewer hours were any less worthy of the things that are basic to life. What God gives, God intends to be shared with all, so that the needs of all are met. And God's own grace is the ultimate judgment upon people, and systems, that practice rationing, that promote resentment, that protect privilege.

What is "justice"? Jesus said, "Let me tell you a story about the kingdom of heaven."

Twenty-sixth Sunday in Ordinary Time

Spanish Springs Presbyterian Church, Sparks, Nevada

September 26, 1999

Exodus 17:1–7
Philippians 2:1–13
Matthew 21:23–32

"The Way Christians Count"

It seems that the epistle readings from the lectionary for the past several weeks have been addressing very practical aspects of life in the church. They have frankly admitted the *obstacles* to living in harmony with one another in the community of faith, but they have also boldly insisted on the *necessity* of living in harmony with one another in the community of faith. In the closing chapters of Romans, and now again in Philippians, Paul comments on divisions or *potential* divisions within Christian congregations.

In fact, *most* of Paul's letters seem to have been prompted by some dispute and division, or were written anticipating some disagreement and dissension. A cynic might point to this as proof that the Christian cause is futile, and that Christ's commands are irrelevant. An agnostic might consider such evidence as good reason to withhold commitment to the Christian faith. But the *hopeful* person, while confessing that there *is* a human tendency toward divisions, might detect the workings of God's grace through the history of the people of God who, though frequently contentious, though frequently shifting their focus away from Jesus Christ, have never been abandoned by God. The

"The Way Christians Count"

trusting person will give thanks that God has never permitted the church's *very human quarrels* to defeat the church's *very divine purpose*.

All of Paul's writings were occasional in nature—that is, some event prompted the apostle to communicate in a particular way at a particular time with the churches he had established or for which he felt responsible. The letters are pastoral, not dogmatic, and where Paul delivers doctrine, he doesn't mean it to be comprehensive and exhaustive, but he relates it to a particular situation that has arisen in a particular congregation. We contemporary Christians can profit greatly from Paul's letters, and we should seek guidance within them for the Christian life today. But to the extent that we use Paul's letters in a *dogmatic* way with regard to specific issues in our own time, we run the risk of distorting the great apostle's intention and limiting the gospel of Christ.

Part of the difficulty we run into as we read Paul's letters is that we cannot know precisely what the debates in the New Testament churches were all about. After all, we only have one side of the correspondence. In the case of the church at Philippi in Macedonia, part of what is now Greece, we *do* know that Paul felt a sincere affection for the congregation as he was addressing them from a prison cell. The Philippian congregation had sent him some sort of gift, and he was writing a thank-you letter to express his gratitude. And in the letter, he also informed the congregation of his hopeful state of heart and mind in prison. But alongside the abiding serenity and joy that Paul felt even in *prison*, he was grieved and anxious at hearing, perhaps from the very courier who had delivered the gift, that there was grumbling contention in the congregation. The fourth chapter of Philippians refers to a jealous argument between two church members; some scholars suppose that it was threatening to split the congregation.

But things need not have been that extreme. It is just as likely that it was a general mood of petty bickering that disturbed Paul and that, while not unusual in congregations, was hindering the proper fulfillment of mission within this church that Paul loved so deeply and for which he prayed so fervently. "If then there is any encouragement in Christ," Paul wrote (and Paul clearly believed that there *is*), "any consolation from love, any sharing in the Spirit, any compassion and sympathy, make my joy *complete*: be of the *same mind*, having the *same love*, being in *full accord* and of *one mind*" (Phil 2:1–2, NRSV). With such resources as Christ within them and the Spirit to sustain them and God's love to bind them, how could *any* Christians give in to rancor and division? Rivalry, jealousy, competition, and accusation have no place in the fellowship of believers. Even the most common pettiness could have disastrous consequences of cosmic proportions when it came to the matter of

Twenty-sixth Sunday in Ordinary Time

faithfully reflecting Christ to one another and giving witness to Christ in the world. The root of the woes of the church was self-centeredness, always a danger and especially destructive when it is disguised in the garb of piety. Paul's prescription for *curing* the righteous competitiveness and holy turf wars at Philippi: "Do nothing from selfish ambition or conceit, but in humility regard others as better than yourselves" (Phil 2:3, NRSV), or, in the words of the old Revised Standard Version of the Bible, "*count* others as better than yourselves" (Phil 2:3b, RSV).

Of all the attempts to turn the teachings of Paul into *requirements* for living, I think that I have never heard a Christian declare that Christians are not as good as *other* people. I have frequently heard just the *opposite*—the unscriptural and self-righteous claim that Christians are *better* than others—but no theologian or church member has ever so tortured Philippians as to make it into a doctrine of Christian inferiority. And of course, Paul is not teaching any such doctrine here. But Paul *is* providing sound advice for solving the problems of quarreling and division in the Philippian church. And his advice is based on his conviction that Christians must imitate in their own lives the Christ whom they profess as Lord: "Let the same mind be in you that was in Christ Jesus, who, though he was in the form of God, did not regard *equality* with God as something to be exploited, but emptied himself, taking the form of a slave, being born in human likeness. And being found in human form, he humbled himself and became obedient to the point of death—even death on a cross" (Phil 2:5–8, NRSV).

Humility is something easily cast aside when a person believes that he or she is engaged in an important work and is giving up his or her time and perhaps material wealth in the process. Humility certainly could not have come naturally to Paul. He had surrendered nearly everything for the sake of spreading the gospel far from home and amidst all sorts of dangers. And on top of that, he had been trained as one who was considered to be spiritually *superior* to others—a *Pharisee*, scrupulous in personal observance of the law, vigilant that others should observe the law in its particulars, quick with judgment upon all who fell short of the law's standards, and careful to avoid any contact with such people. But through the grace of God and the example of Christ and the discipline of the Spirit, Paul the Christian managed to submerge his earlier pridefulness—at least on *most* occasions—and could perceive how out of place pridefulness *is* for a follower of Jesus, who was an obedient servant even to death. Even *minor* instances of pridefulness, Paul came to realize, could have devastating effects within a community of faith. In *larger* doses, it could even put the Son of God on a cross. Paul must have been chagrined to realize that *he* had been just the sort of person with whom Jesus

"The Way Christians Count"

had been in greatest conflict during his ministry, those who made a great show of saying "yes" to God, but then, like the second son in the parable, disobeyed their Father with their gossip and their vanity and their hatred and their lack of mercy. They had rejected the genuine righteousness of *John* who was not so proud as to turn away tax collectors and harlots. They had rejected *Jesus* in the same way, and after his death, they sought out the *disciples* of Jesus to *destroy* them because the pure hearts of the *disciples* put their *own* legalistic purity to shame.

It is an irony of history that the one religion that centers on perfect servanthood should experience its first twenty centuries of growth within a culture which does not regard humility as a virtue. Neither the Greeks nor the Romans, nor the barbarian tribes of northern and eastern Europe, nor indeed their descendants transplanted in the Americas, much taught humility; quite the opposite. Our education from the cradle on in the West has generally been about "success" and "advancement" and how to push *ahead* of others. And it may just be that our civilization's failure to value and practice humility—to count *others* as better than *ourselves*, or at least as *equals*—is finally about to *destroy* community in the Western world. Our disagreements and our self-assertiveness seem to have reached a new level of ugliness in the political arena and the social realm and even in the churches. Racism and nationalism have been rising again in Europe and America, and nativism is certainly apparent in many places. In the very Western civilization which has historically considered itself to be based on Bible teachings, our debates more and more are being waged with slander, shooting, burning, bombing, and some people say with a straight face that the *holiness* of their cause, whatever it might be, *justifies* such behavior. At least one popular Christian program of lay pastoral care includes training in self-assertiveness. We have a right to make demands, it seems to say, an obligation to "look out for number one." And then we wonder why Christians can't always seem to get along!

Of course, each one of us counts in God's eyes, and counts deeply. And our opinions and our needs should count in the church. But the church of Jesus Christ does not exist for our pleasure, or for our convenience, or for our self-satisfaction, but for the purpose of glorifying God in Jesus Christ. I think that we have often ignored the context of the second chapter of Philippians so that we have failed to notice that its words about humility are not just a description of who *Jesus* was, but a declaration of who *we* are to be. The way the Christian counts is not to exalt oneself, not to assert oneself, not to push oneself to the fore, but to count *others* as *better* than ourselves, looking to *their* interests at least as much as our own. In our quiet confidence in God's love for us, we do not have to prove the importance of our discipleship to others or even to ourselves. The way *Christians* count is to empty ourselves, and take

Twenty-sixth Sunday in Ordinary Time

the role of servants, submerging pride, forgetting self, eager to please God by ministering to humankind in the manner and in the name of Jesus Christ the living Lord.

"Therefore, my beloved," wrote Paul to the congregation so dear to him as he was imprisoned far from them and sensing that he might not live to see them again, "just as you have always obeyed me, not only in my presence, but much more now in my absence, work out your own salvation with fear and trembling" (Phil 2:12, NRSV). That means to live in remembrance of our mortal weakness and in sole reliance upon the grace of God, who values us and every person so much that he sent his only Son to live and die and live again for our salvation. Unity in mind, solidarity in love, being in full accord—that is the will of God not only for the Christians in Philippi two thousand years ago, but for the Presbyterian Christians in Spanish Springs today. Of course, such total humility as all *that* requires would be impossible, were we to have to rely upon our own will and our own resources. But do not despair of growing up into the humility of Christ, says Paul, who had himself experienced so great a transformation from pridefulness to servanthood. "[F]or it is *God* who is at work in *you*, *enabling* you both to will and to work for *his* good pleasure" (Phil 12:13, NRSV).

Twenty-seventh Sunday in Ordinary Time

Spanish Springs Presbyterian Church, Sparks, Nevada

October 5, 2008

Exodus 20:1–4, 7–9, 12–20
Philippians 3:4b–14
Matthew 21:33–46

"Grateful for Salvation"

About fifteen years ago, I attended a summer class at a seminary that has a reputation for theological conservatism. I had registered for the course through the Vancouver School of Theology, which is a joint institution of the Anglican Church of Canada and the United Church of Canada, and affiliated with the Presbyterian Church in Canada, but the class itself was being offered as part of the summer school curriculum of Regent College, a few blocks down the street. I understand that it has some affiliation with Pat Robertson. The title of the course was "Law and Grace." My interest in it had been stimulated by debates over sexuality, specifically whether ordination as ministers, elders, and deacons in the Presbyterian Church (USA) should be open to homosexual persons. Believe it or not, that was a topic that created some controversy in the national church fifteen years ago. Of course, the subject matter of the class was much broader than that specific question, but my particular motivation for traveling from Dodge City, Kansas, to Vancouver, British Columbia, was to engage in serious doctrinal study in the entire theological area of scriptural law and God's gracious dealing with people traditionally judged to be sinners

Twenty-seventh Sunday in Ordinary Time

as preparation for tackling that specific and very emotional issue in congregations and judicatories.

The instructor for the course was a seminary professor from Scotland—how much more Reformed could you *get*? The curriculum was built around reading and discussing the works of the nineteenth-century churchman, John McLeod Campbell—again, how much more Scottish, and Reformed, could you *get*? Toward the end of the course, the professor made the observation that, according to scripture (and Mr. Campbell), God's gift of *grace* always comes before God's *command*; *salvation* always precedes the *law*. Immediately, hands shot up all around me. The Regent College students objected strenuously to the assertion that God acts graciously in saving us before commanding us not to break the laws that God lays down, that God *welcomes* before imposing a *duty*. The professor held his ground, though he obviously lost the respect of many who had been lapping up all that he had previously said about God's righteous judgment of sinners and the peril in which violators of the law place themselves. Theirs was the popular view of sin and salvation, which apparently had been nurtured in their other classes at that institution as well as their churches and parachurches. In *this* instance, at least, the theology that they had learned did not match the testimony of the Bible. (In the spirit of full disclosure, let me acknowledge that Campbell himself was judged guilty of heresy in 1831 by the General Assembly of the Church of Scotland for holding that Christ died for all, not just for a "predestined" few.) To put it simply, Campbell (and this professor) were arguing, on the basis of scripture, that we do not need God's *salvation* because we have *broken* God's *law*. Rather, we follow God's *law* because we have *experienced* God's *salvation*. And in *that*, the leaders of the Reformation were agreed. That is why, for instance, the Heidelberg Catechism teaches the meaning of the Ten Commandments under the heading, "Thankfulness."

The Israelites did not receive the Ten Commandments and all the other of God's laws that Moses delivered to them until God had already saved them from their slavery in Egypt. And the reason that God *gave* the commandments and all the other laws Moses spoke about was for the purpose of forming a community for himself and that would be a blessing to others. The laws laid down in Exodus, Leviticus, Numbers, and Deuteronomy—sometimes together referred to as the "Law of Moses"—describe how a people who have been *saved* by God, and who acknowledge God as *their* God, and who therefore want to *please* God, are to *live*. It was as a people grateful for what God had *already done* for them that they would obey the Ten Commandments and all the other instructions for life in the covenant community God had formed—and the word "instructions" is really a more descriptive term for them than "laws."

"Grateful for Salvation"

The first words of what we know as the Ten Commandments are not only an introduction to the instructions written down on two tablets of stone. They are the introduction to the whole *collection* of instructions that Moses laid before the people on God's behalf: "I am the LORD your God, who brought you out of the land of Egypt, out of the house of slavery" (Exod 20:2, NRSV). It is because of that historical fact, with all of its implications—social and political as well as religious—that the Israelites and their spiritual ancestors were to behave in the way that all the succeeding verses and chapters of the Pentateuch, the Torah, specify. Moses proclaimed that proper behavior includes not only the things we can enumerate on ten fingers, but all the *other* instructions in the Torah, including not eating shellfish, for instance, and not loaning money at interest.

The law is an instrument of a mutual relationship between God and God's people. Keeping the law—following the instructions—is the way that faith-full people respond to God's love. Doing what God *commands*, and refraining from what God *prohibits*, is the way in which people who know themselves to have been *saved* express their gratitude to God for God's saving deeds, including God's act of salvation in Jesus Christ. To fail to do what is commanded, and to do the things that are prohibited, is to declare oneself as being outside the covenant community that God has established by saving a people and calling them to himself—a community that God has opened up beyond the biological children of Abraham by the resurrection of Christ and the gift of the Holy Spirit and the commission to go and make disciples of all nations, breaking down every boundary of race, nation, and class, propelling the tide of God's salvation and making way for a great swell of thanksgiving that carries the whole world to the shores of God's new creation.

No one is saved by keeping the law. We cannot earn salvation. We will never deserve it. Our salvation is the result *only* of Christ's obedient death on the cross. But no one who understands that Christ's obedient death on the cross has *saved* them could possibly want to *violate* the law. The law is the description of how a people who know that they have been redeemed will live. And that understanding should have a fundamental influence on the way we regard the Ten Commandments and all the other do's and don'ts of the Bible, and on the way we discuss important issues in church and in society.

The traditional approach of the revivalist preacher and the street-corner evangelist has been to tell people that they are sinners for breaking the law, and that they need salvation from their sins, usually thought of as specific actions that violate particular commandments. But the apostle Paul realized that the need for salvation is more systemic than that, more basic, more rooted in the human condition. As far as Paul was aware—and he was pretty confident in this—he had not violated any of the law. He kept the commandments. He observed the rituals. He was as close to *perfect* as anybody could *be* perfect in fulfilling the do's and don'ts of the Bible. He would have been unfazed by the revivalist preacher or the street-corner evangelist. His observance of every jot and tittle of the law, the actions that he did and refrained from doing, was punctilious. As far as anyone could have graded him on a scorecard, he was flawless. "If anyone else has reason to be confident in the flesh"—that is, in the realm of human attainment and human values—"*I* have *more*: circumcised on the eighth day" (which is what the law specifies), "a member of the people of Israel, of the tribe of Benjamin, a Hebrew born of Hebrews" (even better than one's ancestors having come over on the Mayflower); "as to the law, a Pharisee" (the self-appointed keepers of the law and judges of whether *other* people were keeping it or not); "as to zeal, a persecutor of the church" (which Jews would generally have considered defending the holiness of God); "as to righteousness under the law, blameless" (he fulfilled all the commandments) (Phil 3:4b–6, NRSV). No one, under the accepted standards of behavior, would have considered Paul a *sinner*.

And yet, of course, he *was*. *Not* because he had broken the *law*, but because, despite his *keeping* the law, in fact because he was so *good* at keeping the law, he *wasn't*, perhaps *couldn't* be, thankfully dependent upon *God*. He could describe every tree in the forest, and yet, he was blind to the forest itself—until, that is, while on an errand to make sure that everyone else was keeping the law, the risen Lord Jesus Christ knocked him to his knees with a flash of light. "[W]hatever gains I had," Paul testified to his fellow Christians at Philippi, "these I have come to regard as *loss* because of Christ. More than that, I regard *everything* as loss because of the surpassing value of knowing Christ Jesus my Lord" (Phil 3:7–8a, NRSV). Knowing *Christ* was Paul's salvation, *not* keeping the *law*. "For his sake I have suffered the loss of all things," presumably including his collection of good citizenship awards,

> and I regard them as *rubbish*, in order that I may gain *Christ* and be found in *him*, *not* having a righteousness of my own that comes from the *law*, but one that comes through *faith* in *Christ*, the righteousness from God based on faith. I want to know Christ and the power of his resurrection and the sharing of his sufferings by becoming like him in his death, if somehow I may attain the resurrection from the dead.
>
> Not that I have already obtained this or have already reached the goal; but I press on to make it my *own*, because Christ Jesus has made me *his* own. Beloved, I do not consider that I have made it my own; but this one thing I do: forgetting what lies behind and

"Grateful for Salvation"

straining forward to what lies ahead, I press on toward the goal of the prize of the heavenly call of God in Christ Jesus. (Phil 3:8b–14, NRSV)

Keeping the law so well all those years had not delivered Paul at life's goal; in that race for the finish line he had no advantage over the most wretched of human beings. Salvation came through faith in Jesus Christ crucified and risen, and gratitude for Jesus Christ crucified and risen was the only pertinent motivation for keeping the law. Once, Paul had interpreted obedience to God as a function of the law. The result had been to regard external observances as preeminent; to mistake detail for substance; to divide people into categories of superior and inferior, acceptable and unacceptable; to replace allegiance to the living God with enslavement to words in a book; to emphasize his own ability to think and act over gratitude for the wonder of divine grace. No one is *righteous* but by the mercy of *God*. No one is *saved* but by the cross of *Jesus Christ*.

That is why what will happen at this table in a few minutes is so extraordinary. That is why every Sunday should be World Communion Sunday. This sign and seal of our salvation speaks of the nature of salvation itself, and the more frequently we come to this table, the more likely we are to recognize that our salvation lies somewhere and in someone beyond our own ability. Like salvation itself, this dinner is neither earned nor deserved. It is not a private possession or a certificate suitable for framing. It is a meal open to all, a generous gift from the hand of God and hosted by the living Lord Jesus Christ. It is not a ritual for the perfect, but a reminder of dependence, equally one and all, on the grace of the one who created and sustains all living things. Take and eat, and so taste and see, not *your* goodness nor *mine*, but the goodness of the Lord. And then live as people who are grateful for your salvation.

Twenty-eighth Sunday in Ordinary Time

Spanish Springs Presbyterian Church, Sparks, Nevada

October 13, 2002

Exodus 32:1–14
Philippians 4:1–9
Matthew 22:1–14

"No Business as Usual"

Her majesty Queen Elizabeth II has been touring Canada this past week in celebration of the Golden Jubilee of her reign. Her first stop was the far northern native village of Iqaluit, where the days are already short and the parkas are within easy reach. With a smile, she received flowers and letters of greeting from people who broke through the security line in Winnipeg. She even threw down the puck to start a hockey game in Vancouver. It seems that the queen is rubbing the royal shoulders with the common people in her Commonwealth in a rather more familiar way than she ever did prior to the death of Lady Diana. As a result, she is receiving some of the special affection that the public felt toward her mother, who always managed to retain a bit of the common touch. For so many years, Elizabeth's reign has been built upon traditional observance of the formal distinction between royalty and commoners, an emotional distance that struck many people as positively un-human in times of family tragedy and national crisis. Her formality is softening a bit, and it may just be enough of an adaptation to keep the British monarchy going for another generation.

"No Business as Usual"

We in this country don't know as much about these things, of course. And the headlines of impending warfare abroad and more horrible gun murders at home have eclipsed any mention of the queen's visit to the country next door in our morning headlines or on our evening newscasts. But we probably know enough about royalty that we would be impressed to receive a dinner invitation to the palace of a queen or a king. I would think that any of us would immediately drop what we were doing, clear the calendar, and lay out our best clothes, perhaps even buy some *new* ones, in order to dine with royalty. Surely, the same thing would have been true in ancient times.

So when Jesus told his parable about the king who invited guests to a wedding banquet in honor of his son, his listeners would no doubt have been amazed that the guests, when the day of the party arrived, refused, each and every one, to attend. "[T]hey made light of it and went away, one to his farm, another to his business, while the rest seized [the king's] slaves, mistreated them, and killed them" (Matt 22:5–6, NRSV). In *Matthew's* telling of the story, not only were the guests extremely rude and disrespectful, but they were murderously treasonous, as well. Quite understandably, "[t]he king was enraged" (Matt 22:7a, NRSV). He sent his soldiers to execute swift and ultimate justice upon the murderers and even ordered that they burn down their cities—punishing not just the ungrateful guests, but everyone who had anything to do with them.

Now, the dinner had already been prepared—the oxen and fatted calves had been slaughtered; the meat was going to go to waste if there was no one to eat it. And his son's wedding, of course, still deserved to be celebrated. "The wedding is ready," the king said to his slaves, "but those invited were not worthy" (Matt 22:8b, NRSV). Jesus' hearers would have recognized the dilemma and wondered what was going to happen next. They were undoubtedly surprised by the king's solution: "Go therefore into the main streets, and invite everyone you find to the wedding banquet" (Matt 22:9, NRSV).

Many of us saw the royal weddings of Princes Charles, Andrew, and Edward on television. We remember the pomp and the pageantry and the gala, the tuxedos and the uniforms and the gowns, the millions of people lining the parade routes and all of the city of Westminster shut down for the occasion. Can you picture the queen's disappointment and amazement if the guests invited to the actual wedding and dinner party had *ignored* the invitations because they considered it more important to take a trip to the farm or putter about the office? Can you picture the mob scene if the queen had instructed her staff to open the gates of Buckingham Palace and the doors of the dining hall to the crowd out on the streets? Preposterous, you say! But in the story that Jesus told, "[t]hose slaves went out into the streets and gathered all whom

Twenty-eighth Sunday in Ordinary Time

they found, both good and bad; so the wedding hall was filled with guests" (Matt 22:10, NRSV). We can just imagine that some of them were swinging from the chandeliers.

To the basic story, which Luke also included in *his* Gospel in a somewhat different form, Matthew added the king's judgment against someone who came in off of the street improperly attired. But the main point of the parable surely has to do with the failure of the original invited guests to come to the dinner, offering as their reason their need to go about their business as usual, and Jesus' audience's shock that anyone would pass up such an invitation, or that the king would thereupon open the doors to the riff-raff.

In the Kerygma class on parables that some of us are attending currently on Tuesday afternoons and Wednesday evenings, we have learned that the parables of Jesus are stories rich with meaning and multifaceted in their truth. It so happens that the parable of the wedding banquet was one of the stories featured in this past week's lesson. It has such depth, and there are so many ways of looking at it, that no single sermon could possibly exhaust its meaning. But something that I noticed, both in Matthew's version and in Luke's, is the way in which the invited guests thought nothing wrong with going about their regular business as usual instead of responding to the invitation to the great banquet. And compared with attending the king's wedding feast for his son, the prince, business as usual was a very trivial pursuit—going out to the farm, checking in at the office. They had known about the banquet for days, had presumably already indicated they would attend, but when the time actually came to feast and celebrate, they decided they had better things to do.

We must be careful not to allegorize the parables—not to say that *this* stands for one thing, and *that* stands for something else—but Jesus introduced the story as a parable of the kingdom of heaven. So the kingdom of heaven is like a big party to which some who have been invited and have said all along they intend to take advantage of, at the last minute, when the day that they have been waiting for actually arrives, decide that it isn't worth their time, and so *their* place at the table is given instead to people who never thought themselves qualified even to receive an *invitation*. The wedding hall has been prepared for a party, and the king will fill it one way or another, so that his generosity doesn't go to waste. So it is with God. The kingdom of heaven is being prepared for you and me. We have said that we *want* a seat at the table, maybe even *expect* a seat at the table. But the question is put to *us* in Jesus' parable: when the time comes to step into the banquet hall, will we do so with joy, or will we decide after all that we prefer to go about our business as usual? And when we consider the fact that the kingdom of heaven isn't just a destination after death, but a living reality here and now for anyone who is in Christ Jesus,

"No Business as Usual"

the choice between the joy of the kingdom and pursuing the trivia of business as usual is one that can come at any moment, and, in fact, *does*.

The apostle Paul wanted his converts to Christianity to live always in preparation for the return of Christ. He expected it would be imminent. He didn't want anyone to miss out on the opportunity of being with Christ for eternity. But he also believed that we *can* and *should* have life in Christ even *now*, in our daily activities and relationships and attitudes and expectations. "Rejoice in the Lord always," he wrote to the Christians at Philippi; "again I will say, Rejoice" (Phil 4:4, NRSV). And that consciousness of being in Christ had implications for behavior. "Let your gentleness be known to everyone" (Phil 4:5a, NRSV). It also had signaled a readiness for the destiny every Christian says he or she desires. "The Lord is near," said Paul (Phil 4:5b, NRSV). So, everything about the present was transformed in anticipation of Christ's sudden appearance—the doors of the banquet hall suddenly being flung open for the long-awaited feast. There could be no business as usual—because the *un*usual was about to happen. "Do not worry about anything, but in everything by prayer and supplication with thanksgiving let your requests be made known to God" (Phil 4:6, NRSV). Nothing could compare with the importance of responding to the invitation when the moment arrived; ordinary worries and anxieties and occupations couldn't compare with the *extra*ordinary blessings and joys and rewards of faithfulness to Christ's summons. "And the peace of God, which surpasses all understanding, will guard your hearts and your minds in Christ Jesus" (Phil 4:7, NRSV).

On a day-to-day basis, you and I have to tend to the plowing and the planting and the weeding and the harvesting on the farm, you and I have to tend to the reading and writing and problem-solving and test-taking in school, you and I have to tend to the correspondence and decision-making in the office and the craftsmanship and filling of orders in the shop. But, on a day-to-day basis, for you and me, those pursuits have been transformed into something far from trivial—they are opportunities to serve others, to forgive others, to pray for others, to rejoice in God's generosity and trust in God's promise and experience God's peace.

You and I are in Christ. We already have a foot in the kingdom. We already have the invitation in our hands. And in our daily comings and goings, the summons is ever before us to live as citizens of the kingdom of heaven, to occupy our place at the banquet table, by committing ourselves to whatever is true, whatever is honorable, whatever is just, whatever is pure, whatever is pleasing, whatever is commendable, whatever is excellent and worthy of praise. No spite, no hatred, no greed, no dishonesty, no revenge, no selfishness, even though the kingdom of the world may seem to reward such things, may seem to expect such things, may seem to thrive on such things, may seem to require such things of us. At the last minute, when, with a word spoken or a deed done, or a word *un*spoken or a deed *un*done, *we* have the option of entering fully into the kingdom of heaven or deciding that the invitation just isn't worth it, we face the choice of whether we will participate in God's new order of peace and justice and mercy which already *is* but is not *yet*—which already *is* in the certainty of God's will, but which is not *yet* in the *un*certainty of our decision. It is not a matter of how faithful we are at going to church (though I don't in any way want to discourage it), or how much we read the Bible (though I don't in any way want to discourage it), or how much we pray (though I don't in any way want to discourage it). It is about how willing we are to let go of the securities and promises and comforts and habits of the world, and enter into the securities and promises and comforts and habits of the kingdom of heaven—the peace and justice and mercy for which we may rejoice in the Lord always. It's about how clearly we recognize Jesus Christ standing before us all day every day, continuously bidding us into the great feast of joy and salvation that, one day, will be a party without end.

It is so easy to want our satisfactions in a form that we can take to the bank, so to speak—to follow the golden calves of family and occupation and health and fortune and fame and popularity. The invitation to the king's banquet, so far in the future, can be put in the drawer and forgotten amidst the competing concerns that crowd our calendars and claim our attention. But Jesus says that the joy that the *world* offers and the joy that the *kingdom of heaven* offers are not even worth comparing.

I imagine that those who were fortunate enough to have had invitations to the various social gatherings on the queen's itinerary this past week will remember the event for the rest of their lives. I am sure that not one of them would trade it for what they might have accomplished that day on the farm or in the office. The kingdom of heaven, Jesus said, is like a party to which a king has invited guests, but, when the day arrives, the invited guests decide not to respond, but instead go on with business as usual. Unbelievable! But then, their unwise choice provides an opportunity for unexpected joy for those who never imagined that *they* might be on the guest list, and they *immediately* drop whatever *they're* doing to take advantage of such great generosity. God's invitation to the kingdom of heaven—the peace and mercy and joy that the world's promises and allegiances and rewards cannot offer—is not something to pass up in favor of business as usual—the worries and anxieties and preoccupations of chasing our own salvation. God's invitation to the kingdom of heaven is an invitation to life in Christ Jesus. The doors are open to joy and mercy and peace without end. And the King has reserved a place for you.

Twenty-ninth Sunday in Ordinary Time

Spanish Springs Presbyterian Church, Sparks, Nevada

October 19, 2008

Exodus 33:12–23
1 Thessalonians 1:1–10
Matthew 22:15–22

"The Glory of God"

Pietro Sabatini looked out of the window of his studio toward the great dome of the cathedral on the far side of the river. Once again, as happened at some point nearly every day for the past twelve years, his mind came back to the way in which he had once disobeyed God, had shown his lack of faith in God, had argued with God late into the night. Life had become harder for him since that night. It wasn't that people didn't like his paintings. He had become more renowned for his work nearly every year. Some of the city's leading families had commissioned him to paint portraits. His landscapes had won praise from his peers. He could command top price for his efforts. He was popularly regarded as a genius, and was compared favorably with the great artists of the past. He was especially sought out by priests and bishops to produce masterpieces for the church.

But the more he painted, especially religious themes, the deeper was his gnawing discomfort with himself. Perhaps it was because he painted so many religious themes that there was within him a growing sense that he must honor God with an exquisite piece of art that would be the supreme accomplishment of his life and set a new standard for other fine artists to emulate. It was not

Twenty-ninth Sunday in Ordinary Time

that he wanted more human praise, although that was always welcome, of course. No, he wanted to please God, perhaps atone for his brash impudence that night a dozen years earlier. There was no excuse for what he had said to God. Provocation, yes—the circumstances of his anger—but, he knew in the pit of his soul, no excuse. He had always tried to be a pious person, obeying the commandments as the priests explained them, giving alms when he could, taking the host when it was offered, donating some of the pictures he painted for churches when it seemed especially appropriate to do so. But he remained deeply conscious of his offense against God.

For some months now, a plan of penance had been forming in his mind. He would paint the face of God. He knew that such a proposal was filled with risk—risk on the religious side (the church's teaching against trying to portray God was stern, if inconsistent—look at Michelangelo's own great fresco on the ceiling of the Sistine Chapel, which, a century-and-a-half now after the great artist's crowning achievement, was universally hailed as inspired), risk on the professional side (to attempt such a task and to fail—he would be a laughingstock among his contemporaries and ridiculed or pitied through all time to come). Today, he thought, he must make a decision. There were several commissions that had been proposed to him; would he put them off in favor of giving his full attention to this more daunting task? If he did not, he feared his courage might desert him. He must do it now or never. Actually, he had been suspecting for weeks that he must make a decision. But now that the moment had come, he realized, he did not have the inspiration that would be necessary. All he had was a sense of penitence. His mind had not conceived any way of communicating, on canvas, the absolute and total glory of God. No colors on his palette were vibrant enough. No tones in his pigments were rich enough. No countenance he could imagine was holy enough. No scheme of composition was perfect enough.

The artist turned from the large window and sat heavily in a chair, his paint-stained smock mimicking the capes of cardinals and nobles who had sat there to cast approval or disapproval on his efforts—mostly approval, thankfully. He bowed his head and clasped his hands in his lap. "O, Lord, how shall I reveal your glory to the world? How shall I see you and make you known? Communicate yourself to me, let my eyes feast upon your holiness, that I may glorify you as none other has ever done." And he continued to sit there for nearly an hour, but no image came before his mind's eye. Eventually, he sighed deeply, exchanged his smock for a morning jacket, took his cane in his hand, and descended the three flights of steps to the street below.

He had frequently strolled the streets of the city looking into the faces of its inhabitants for inspiration for his paintings. He often worked with models,

"The Glory of God"

but, before he called upon a model, he would customarily search the traffic of the markets and the piazzas and even the churches identifying types for the picture he was painting. Even when he was painting portraits, his study of faces in the street gave him insight into expression and mood. He was walking now toward the river and the stalls where vendors hawked their wares. He had vaguely in mind a route that would eventually take him to the piazza in front of the cathedral where he might even enter the great church itself and search a past generation's efforts to honor God for inspiration how he might achieve perfection where they had fallen short. His sense of urgency was great, and yet he knew from long experience that artistic inspiration could not be conjured up on demand. But surely God could understand the depth of his desire to draw attention not to himself, but to God. Would God not be eager to help in such a great enterprise, to assist the artist in showing forth his glory in its fullness?

With such thoughts in his head, Pietro Sabatini had unconsciously come to a halt halfway across the bridge that was lined with vendors' stalls. "For your sideboard, sir?" The question seemed to break into his awareness from out of the blue. "Flowers?" the voice persisted. A teenaged girl was holding out a bouquet assortment of blooms in front of him. "Picked fresh this morning, signor."

"What? No, no, not today."

"But they are beautiful, are they not?"

"Yes, quite, but I'm in a hurry. I'm on a mission."

The girl's eyelids drooped.

"I'm sorry. Not today." And he pressed on through the crowded passage.

When he emerged from the bridge on the other side of the river, the sound of a bell pealing from the tower above the city hall and echoing through the thoroughfare caught him unawares. "One o'clock," he said to himself, instinctively pulling out his pocket watch and confirming that it was in agreement with the public timepiece. He turned into a trattoria and seated himself at a small, empty table. The proprietor soon made his way through the gathering lunch crowd and inquired how he might serve the gentleman. "Soup and bread," he responded. "And wine." The man nodded and disappeared amidst the small jumble of tables, appearing again in a few minutes with the requested fare. The artist first sipped the wine and then tasted of the soup. Both were satisfactory, and the latter appeared to be more nutritious than the average. He broke off a piece of bread and ate it, at the same time studying the faces of the patrons seated near him, filing away in his mind the features of their expressions for retrieval when they might be useful for a crowd scene or as a characteristic to incorporate into a portrait. The trattoria was noisy and smoky, several of his fellow countrymen having acquired the practice of using the tobacco that was now being imported from the Americas and Anatolia. The artist hastened to finish his meal and resume his walk, but, as he reached into his vest pocket to retrieve a coin to pay for his meal, he was chagrined to discover that his pocket was empty, save for his watch. He had left his apartment without checking first to see whether he had any money with him. The proprietor was now standing expectantly at the artist's table. "I'm terribly sorry," the artist said. "This is most vexing. I seem to have left home without any money upon my person."

The proprietor looked disconsolately at the empty glass and plate and bowl.

"I can bring payment tomorrow. Will that suffice?"

The man now looked more purposefully at the artist's face. "Are you not Signor Pietro Sabatini?"

"Why, yes, as a matter of fact, I am," the artist said, betraying some embarrassment. Would this be the start of a rumor that he was impoverished, or a parasite?

"You painted that picture of the woman with the alabaster jar, did you not? The one that now hangs in the Church of San Bartolomeo? *My* church?"

"Oh, is that *your* church?" the artist asked with genuine interest, somewhat flattered by the recognition.

"Yes. Such a beautiful painting. So real. So inspiring. And the priest told us that you had been commissioned to paint it by one of our parishioners, but that when he died before it was finished, you simply gave it to the church."

"Well, yes. I feared it would have burdened his widow, and—"

"Please," the proprietor interrupted him. "There is no need for you to bring me any payment for your food."

"But, really, I insist."

"No. If you want to pay for it, give the money to someone on the street who is hungry and in need. That will be payment enough. *More* than enough."

"All right, then," the artist promised. "I will do that." He got up from his table, bowed to the proprietor, and resumed his quest for inspiration about the face of God.

Pietro Sabatini had not progressed very far until he came across an old man sitting under an awning, obviously in need of care, and a young boy holding a cup of water to his lips. The old man took a draft from the cup and smiled at the lad as the boy lowered the cup. "Thank you, Giuseppe," the artist could hear the old man say. "Thank you. You are very good to me."

"The Glory of God"

The artist stopped at a respectful distance, wondering at the boy's tenderness. The boy looked up and saw the artist, and an inquiring look came over his face.

"You are very kind to your grandfather," the artist commented.

"Oh, he is not my grandfather. He lives here in the street, and sometimes beside the river. Only now, I think he is sick."

The artist came closer and looked at the man. "Are you not well, signor?" he asked.

"No," the man said with a weak, tired voice. "The boy is so kind. But I think I am ill." And he coughed. His sunken eyes turned up to the artist briefly, and then he lowered them again and his head rolled toward his left shoulder.

"A physician should see him," the artist told the boy. "Do you know where Via degli Cavalieri is? Just a couple of streets away?"

"Yes," the boy nodded.

"Well, in that street there is a physician named Dr. Gasparini. Would you go fetch him, and tell him that Signor Sabatini, the painter, has need of him?" The artist then instinctively put his fingers in his vest pocket, and just as he remembered having discovered it to be empty at the trattoria, he now felt a hard round disk in the lining. He was puzzled for a few seconds, but then discovered the hole in the bottom of the pocket, through which several coins had slipped. With his other hand on the outside of his vest, he was able to maneuver some of them back into the pocket and thence into his fingers. One of these, he held out to the boy.

"After you have found the doctor, take this to that trattoria back there," he pointed to where he had had his lunch, "and ask for some soup and bread that you can bring to me. No, do that first, *then* go to the doctor. I will stay with your friend."

Giuseppe reappeared several minutes later with the requested items and, as the artist held a spoon up to the old man's lips, the boy went off toward Via degli Cavalieri. The old man was eager for the soup but too weak to swallow it easily. He sputtered a "Thank you" as the artist said, "Not too fast, my friend. Let's do it slowly, so that you do not choke. When did you eat last?"

"Two days ago," the man managed a response. "No, three, I think. I don't remember."

After half a dozen spoonfuls, the artist said, "Let's wait a bit. Make sure your stomach handles that before we give you any more. Then we'll try some bread." After a few moments, he asked, "What was the boy's name again? Do you know who he is?"

Twenty-ninth Sunday in Ordinary Time

The man smiled. "Giuseppe. He is a God-send, that little boy. An orphan, I think, or essentially so. He begs, and then he gives me most of what people give him." The man coughed again. "May I have some more soup?"

"Yes," said the artist, "but not too fast."

Within a few minutes, little Giuseppe came back into sight, followed by Dr. Gasparini. "I feared it was *you* who was ill," the physician said to the artist. "The boy, here, said you had sent for me and that it was urgent."

The boy gazed at the artist, with a look of fear that he had done something wrong. "You did well," the artist assured him, then looked toward the doctor. "Can you care for this man, and I will pay you whatever is owed? I was afraid he could not walk to your house."

"I know a place on this street where he can rest," the physician said. "And I will attend to him. You keep your money and save it up for when I have to treat you for gout," he winked and chuckled. The two men lifted the man up, supporting him on their shoulders, and walked him up the street, Giuseppe following with the soup and bread.

A few minutes later, Pietro Sabatini found himself in the great cathedral, gazing at its marble columns and gilded ornaments and rich mosaics and famous paintings. In one of the side chapels, he saw a woman kneeling in prayer. Her face, from what he could see, interested him, and he moved closer. He could not help overhearing the words she was speaking. "And I am so grateful that he is back, safe and unharmed. I feared I would never see my son again, it had been so long. And when he asked my forgiveness, how my heart overflowed with pity. How can I thank you enough? What can I give you in return for having my son back?" Suddenly conscious of the profound emotions upon which he was eavesdropping, the artist backed away with embarrassment.

He noticed the confessional booth not far away, and walked toward it, cautiously opening the door and stepping inside. "Yes?" came an inquiring voice from beyond the screen.

"Father, I have sinned."

"Yes?" the voice repeated.

"Many years ago, I told God that he had disappointed me in a business venture. And, out of anger toward him and vengeance toward the man with whom I had invested some money, I kept some property the man had entrusted to me and sold it and told him that it had been stolen. I argued with God, I told him that the property was mine by right. And then the man killed himself, and I learned that he had lost all he owned in that business venture. He had not cheated me, as I thought. The enterprise had failed utterly, and he had been ruined by its failure, and it took everything he had."

"The Glory of God"

"And you have been carrying this guilt for many years?" the priest asked from beyond the screen.

"I am an artist. I want to make amends. I intend to paint a marvelous painting and give it to the church. I want to paint the face of God in all its glory."

"But you cannot do that," said the priest. "No one has ever seen God's face. Remember how even Moses had to hide in a cleft in the rock on the holy mountain, and was permitted only to see God's glory after he had passed by, after his goodness has been accomplished. Even when we know God is present, he prefers to remain hidden. And that is for our sake. No, your penance should be to go to the man's family and ask their forgiveness and pay them what you took of the man's property."

"But his wife died shortly after that, and he had no children living."

"Then give generously for the poor," the priest prescribed. "And pray for the rest of the man's soul, and that of his wife."

Pietro Sabatini sat in the chair of his studio. It was now late in the afternoon. The priest's words about the inability to paint the face of God had unsettled him. Perhaps he should give up on his plan, if even the *priest* had questioned it! But he had so wanted to honor God and show forth his glory to everyone. He sighed and fumbled in his vest pocket for his watch. That reminded him that he must get the pocket mended. That, in turn, reminded him of the coin that he had found in the lining, and that reminded him of little Giuseppe.

Suddenly, he sat upright in the chair. "O God, how could I have been so blind?" he said, shaking his head in consternation. "How could I have been so blind?" He walked to his table and pulled a piece of paper in front of him and, taking a pencil, he started sketching a scene.

Exactly one month later, Pietro Sabitini was sitting again in the confessional booth at the cathedral. "Yes?" the priest asked from behind the screen.

"Father, it is me, the artist who was here a month ago."

"Yes, I remember."

"I have left something at the chapel nearby. Please accept it as my gift to the diocese for use as you see fit."

He got up and left the confessional before the priest could respond. But when the priest became aware that the supplicant had left the booth, he emerged from behind his door and walked the short space to the chapel, where he saw a parcel wrapped in brown paper. He picked up the heavy rectangular shape, roughly four feet by five, and unwrapped it. It was a triptych, three framed paintings hinged together, on the left side, a man seated at a table and a waiter placing bread and wine in front of him, on the right side, a

Twenty-ninth Sunday in Ordinary Time

doctor kneeling alongside a patient and a woman kneeling in prayer with tears running down her cheek, and, in the middle, in the most prominent position, a young boy holding a cup up to the lips of a seated old man. And, common to each panel, located somewhere in the composition of each, there were flowers. The priest smiled broadly as he saw the title that had been engraved on a little brass plate tacked on to the frame of the middle panel: "The Glory of God."

Thirtieth Sunday in Ordinary Time

First Presbyterian Church, Ponca City, Oklahoma

October 26, 2014

Deuteronomy 34:1–12
1 Thessalonians 2:1–8
Matthew 22:34–46

"Leadership and Followership"

From time to time, I have received anonymous letters in the mail saying that, as a minister, I have no business preaching to Christians from or about the Old Testament. The letters seem to be mass-produced, and other ministers have told me that they have received the same sort of mail. The coming of Jesus, the letters say, made the Old Testament irrelevant. God is no longer interested in the law, has moved beyond the prophets, has decided to leave behind the people he chose way back when. The Reformed faith, though—the theological heritage passed on by John Calvin and John Knox and Martin Bucer and Huldrich Zwingli and others—insists that the story of God with the *Jews* is *our* story, *too*. We believe that you can't make sense out of the *New* Testament without knowing about the *Old*. Jesus himself said that he came not to *abolish* the law and the prophets, but to *fulfill* them. And the Gospels all insist that *Jesus* was a good *Jew*, who knew the law and the prophets as well as anyone he encountered, who observed the feast days of the Jews and honored their traditions, who used the vocabulary and images of the Old Testament to talk about his own ministry and identity. It is hard to understand how anyone could think, for instance, that Moses is irrelevant to the Christian when the New Testament mentions Moses a total of eighty-two times!

In fact, *Matthew's* Gospel seems to want us to think about *Moses* when we think about *Jesus*. So Matthew tells us that Jesus came up out of Egypt after his parents had taken him there in his infancy to escape the death threats of the wicked King Herod, as baby Moses was cast adrift in the Nile to escape the execution order of wicked Pharaoh and then, as an adult, came up out of Egypt to Palestine. The deeds and sayings of Jesus in Matthew are arranged in five lengthy sections, like the five books of the Law of Moses. Jesus delivers the Beatitudes (which some commentators have observed can be arranged as ten teachings) on a mountain, reminiscent of Moses the law-giver having received the Ten Commandments on Mount Sinai.

Moses was the most important figure in Jewish history, greater than David, greater even than Abraham, working wonders, coaxing the people out of slavery in Egypt through the Red Sea and across the desert finally to the threshold of the promised land, and proclaiming the rules by which God wanted the people to live, interceding so often on their behalf to keep God from giving up on them or abandoning them or destroying them. Moses was uniquely the one with whom the Lord spoke face to face, "as one speaks to a friend" (Exod 33:11, NRSV), the book of Exodus says. Though he lived many centuries before the prophetical books of the Bible were written, the Jews reckon Moses the greatest of the prophets, that is, the greatest of the people who made known the ways and desires of God. He also functioned as priest, as military commander, as judge, almost—we might say—as king. The biblical writer or editor whom scholars refer to as the Deuteronomist summed up his regard for Moses this way: "Never since has there arisen a prophet in Israel like Moses, whom the LORD knew face to face. He was unequaled for all the signs and wonders that the LORD sent him to perform in the land of Egypt, against Pharaoh and all his servants and his entire land and for all the mighty deeds and the terrifying displays of power that Moses performed in the sight of all Israel" (Deut 34:10–12, NRSV). And Christians naturally think ahead to the miracles and signs that *Jesus* did, and how the *mercy* of Jesus freed people, *too*—freed them from the consequences of their sins.

So we are a little perplexed why Moses, after all that, was not permitted to enjoy the triumphant moment of Israel crossing the Jordan over into the land that God had promised these people—the land God had first given to Abraham and Sarah so many generations before. Moses had gone up from the plains on the east side of the Jordan River to the top of Mount Nebo to look west over into the promised land, and "[t]he LORD said to him, 'This is the land of which I swore to Abraham, to Isaac, and to Jacob, saying, "I

"Leadership and Followership"

will give it to your descendants"; I have let you see it with your eyes, but you shall not cross over there'" (Deut 34:4, NRSV). A couple of chapters earlier, this disappointing outcome is explained as Moses' penalty for having broken faith with God among the Israelites at the waters of Meribath-kadesh in the wilderness of Zin. God said that Moses had failed to maintain God's holiness among the Israelites—the same Moses who had destroyed their golden calf. It's not clear to us exactly how, when the people grumbled about being thirsty in the desert, and God directed Moses to take the staff—the same staff that he had used in parting the Red Sea—and strike a rock, that water might flow from it, and Moses *did* so, it was in any way an *unfaithful* act. But that is the reason Deuteronomy gives that Moses, like his brother Aaron who died before him, could not enter the promised land with the people they had led and with whom they had shared hardships while learning to depend upon God. It nevertheless seems odd—the *people* were the ones who grumbled—the same people who had worshiped the golden calf,—but *Moses* is the one who was made to pay the penalty. Perfectly healthy, Moses apparently died simply so that he couldn't enter the promised land.

Here, again, we are reminded of Jesus. It's not a direct correlation, of course, and we certainly couldn't say that Moses' death set the people of Israel right with God, but the death of the great prophet for the sins of the people may well have been in the mind of Isaiah when he wrote about the suffering servant, the Old Testament prophecies that Christians regard as key to understanding the suffering of *Jesus* on behalf of others.

To be chosen as a leader of God's people is not a prize that brings worldly admiration or riches. Moses got no testimonial dinners or certificates of appreciation from the people he led out of slavery and across the desert and delivered safely on the banks of the Jordan, not even a plaque, not even a headstone, as it turned out. The people wept for thirty days when Moses died—he had been their leader for all those forty years, and, although they had constantly complained about him, there must have been a lot of hand-wringing when they didn't have him to complain to anymore ("What will become of us now?")—and then they looked to Joshua to get them across the river. Were it up to Moses all those years ago back at the burning bush, he would probably have preferred to continue herding his father-in-law's sheep rather than suffer the abuses and complaints of the people God had entrusted to him, as well as the discomforts of desert life. But then the people would still be back in Egypt making bricks and suffering the lash, or wandering around in circles in the desert aimless and estranged from God until they either starved or died of thirst or were wiped out by enemies.

Thirtieth Sunday in Ordinary Time

Paul the apostle had been roughed up considerably in Philippi before going on to Thessalonica. "[W]e had already suffered and been shamefully mistreated at Philippi," Paul wrote. "[B]ut . . . we speak, not to please mortals, but to please God who tests our hearts. As you know and as God is our witness, we never came with words of flattery or with a pretext for greed; nor did we seek praise from mortals, whether from you or from others, though we might have made demands as apostles of Christ. But we were gentle among you, like a nurse tenderly caring for her own children" (1 Thess 2:2a, 4b–7, NRSV). Choosing to use compassionate persuasion rather than harsh criticism or punishing threats, Paul's concern always was to convey the truth of God and the atoning death and triumphant resurrection of his Son Jesus Christ, patiently, but without compromising the integrity of the gospel. That, too, fits the definition of a prophet. Most scholars conclude that Paul was executed for his faith, probably in Rome, probably in a gruesome way. Like Jesus his Lord, Paul could only do as his conviction of God's will, bestowed by the Holy Spirit, *compelled* him to do. And, where the soil was good, the seeds that he planted along the way sprouted and took root.

Christian bookstores feature a lot of titles on the subject of Christian leadership. And the people of God today, as in ancient times, need good leaders. But the *Bible's* perspective on leadership focuses much on their *faithfulness*, and what God's leaders have to *forgo*, have to *endure*—which, of course, is the part of Jesus' story that all four of the Gospels and so many of Paul's letters come down to. At that point, the focus pivots. Then, the most pressing question becomes, What is needed to be a good *follower*? The Bible offers some *negative* examples—the grumbling Israelites in the wilderness, the people who rejected Paul, and of course those who decided to rid themselves of Jesus, but even, at times, the disciples themselves who were interested more in their own status, their own privileges—their own justification, we might say—than in following Jesus' example of humble and obedient servanthood. The importance of Christian followership is acknowledged in the vows taken by Presbyterian congregations during the service of installation. Each church member is asked to answer the question, whenever a ruling elder is ordained or installed, "Do we, the members of the church, accept [this person] . . . chosen by God through the voice of this congregation to lead us in the way of Jesus Christ? Do we agree to encourage them, to respect their decisions, and to follow as they guide us, serving Jesus Christ who alone is Head of the Church?"[1] Presbyterians understand that doing these things is a necessary part of discipleship.

---

1. Presbyterian Church, *Book of Occasional Services*, 25.

"Leadership and Followership"

Moses hadn't *needed* the job. Moses hadn't *wanted* the job. Moses hadn't *sought* the job. *His* career choice was much more modest, though far below his potential, as God had discerned. But, sensitive as God is to human needs and human feelings, *Moses'* needs and feelings weren't the *issue*. There was God's stubborn determination that God's people be free of their many enslavements, one of which was being forced to make bricks in Egypt to serve the Egyptian economy. *Moses* had to decide whether he would obey God's summons and continue to obey at every discouraging turn, every resistance, every complaint. And the *people* had to decide whether they would follow, though it meant suspending their enjoyment of what little comforts they had, though it meant suspending their belief in hydrodynamics, though it meant suspending their concentration on their stomachs, though it meant suspending their dependence on a certainty they could see and touch, though it meant suspending their expectation of getting to the promised land quickly and without any inconvenience or personal sacrifice. And *then* they found themselves where God had promised they *would* be.

> The LORD said to [Moses], "This is the land of which I swore to Abraham, to Isaac, and to Jacob, saying, 'I will give it to your descendants'; I have let you see it with your eyes, but you shall not cross over there." Then Moses, the servant of the LORD, died there in the land of Moab, at the LORD's command. He was buried in a valley in the land of Moab, opposite Beth-peor, but no one knows the burial place to this day. Moses was one hundred twenty years old when he died; his sight was unimpaired and his vigor had not abated. The Israelites wept for Moses in the plains of Moab thirty days; then the period of mourning for Moses was ended....
>
> Never since has there arisen a prophet in Israel like Moses, whom the LORD knew face to face. He was unequaled for all the signs and wonders that the LORD sent him to perform in the land of Egypt, against Pharaoh and all his servants and his entire land, and for all the mighty deeds and all the terrifying displays of power that Moses performed in the sight of all Israel. (Deut 34:4–8, 10–12, NRSV)

Thirty-first Sunday in Ordinary Time

Spanish Springs Presbyterian Church, Sparks, Nevada

October 30, 2005

Joshua 3:7–17
1 Thessalonians 2:9–13
Matthew 23:1–12

"Muddy Feet"

One important question in interpreting the Bible is to consider why the biblical writer wrote about a particular subject, and why the people of God have preserved that writing and handed it down from generation to generation. After all, John's Gospel concludes by saying that there were many things that Jesus did *in addition* to the ones reported in the Gospel; "if every one of them were written down," the writer declares, "I suppose that the world itself could not contain the books that would be written" (John 21:25b, NRSV). So why did the writer of the Fourth Gospel choose to include certain episodes from the life and ministry and teachings of Jesus, and not others? Why did generation after generation of faithful people find what *was* chosen worthy of being read and studied and acted upon and passed on to the faithful in other lands and later times? We believe, of course, that the Holy Spirit inspired the writers of the books of the Bible to write *this* and not *that*. But the Holy Spirit surely did not *replace* human judgment on such matters, but *nudged* it, and it seems quite likely that the Holy Spirit used the particular but very real needs and circumstances of the community of the faithful to bring to mind certain stories and sayings and to prompt individuals and communities to commit them to

"Muddy Feet"

writing. So it would probably be fair to say that much of what is in the Bible, and the way it is expressed, has something to do with situations known to the biblical writers and that perhaps troubled them, circumstances that they felt needed to be addressed by recalling particular instances and teachings. And that, in turn, helps us reconstruct the history of the people of God, whether it be hundreds of years before Christ, or within just a few decades after the crucifixion and resurrection.

For instance, in the case of Matthew's Gospel, much of what is in the book points to its having been written sometime after the destruction of Jerusalem by the Roman army in AD 70 and the subsequent scattering of Christians from Palestine into other parts of the Near East. Much of what is in the book points to its having been written in Syria—most likely in Antioch, which was one of the earliest centers of Christianity outside of Palestine—and for a congregation that was learning how to distinguish itself from its Jewish neighbors. Matthew's frequent reports of Jesus' criticism of the leaders of the synagogues and other Jewish officials suggests, to a lot of New Testament scholars, that Matthew's *own* congregation had experienced tension with Jewish leaders, and that its members were nursing the wounds of having been excluded from the synagogues. Remember, the earliest Christians considered themselves to be genuinely and thoroughly Jewish, worshiping the God of Israel alongside other Israelites, proclaiming Jesus to be the Messiah, the Son of David, long forecast by the Old Testament prophets. In such an atmosphere of persecution and prejudice, the Pharisees and the scribes and the synagogue leaders would have been natural targets for Matthew's criticism, finding among the many stories about Jesus and among the many teachings of Jesus those episodes and words that put them in a bad light.

But Matthew's congregation would already have been fully aware of the persecution they had suffered; they hardly needed reminding, though it was doubtless comforting to know that Jesus had suffered persecution before them. Might Matthew in fact have been more interested in warning the leaders of the early Christian church against becoming *like* the Pharisees and the scribes and the leaders of the synagogues—not practicing what *they* taught, placing upon others the burden of following all sorts of intricate and technical rules which were no particular hardship for the rich and the healthy but which were difficult indeed for the sick and the poor, making a spectacle of their pious behavior, expecting honor from the people in the streets for their superior religious knowledge or just plain superiority?

We can easily imagine that it didn't take very long for some people in the churches in Antioch and other places to succumb to pride and prestige and hypocrisy and self-righteousness—the same things that remain serious dangers for Christians today. And, so, Matthew chose, from among the many stories about Jesus and the many teachings of Jesus from which he had to select, those things that he thought were most important for his *own* congregation to know about, often as a precaution, and that other congregations found useful for *their* situations, and so Matthew's Gospel came to be cherished and revered not just in Antioch but in many other places as well, doubly so since it was thought to have been written by one of the original twelve disciples who had known Jesus intimately. For even in the church (I hope this does not come as a shock to anyone, although it must always be a disappointment), egos assert themselves and sensitivities get wounded. What is true of the *modern* church, the letters of Paul make clear, was also true of the *early* church. But when *egos* become more important than *forgiveness*, and *pride* outweighs *humility*, we are following the ways of the *Pharisees*, not the ways of *Christ*. The title "rabbi" means "my great one," or "my lord." So Matthew reminded the Christians of his own acquaintance that none of them should claim or assume superiority over another, quoting Jesus' words to his disciples that none of them should allow himself to be called "rabbi;" Jesus *himself* was the one *genuine* rabbi, the Messiah, but even *he* was in fact a *servant*—the truest and most faithful servant of all. "The greatest among you," Jesus said, "will be your servant" (Matt 23:11, NRSV). That is, true greatness is to be found in deeds of lowliness and humility and self-effacement. "All who exalt themselves will be humbled, and all who humble themselves will be exalted" (Matt 23:12, NRSV).

The Gospels often class the chief priests with the scribes and the Pharisees and sometimes the Sadducees as opponents of Jesus, as the *opposite* of what *Jesus* was. Actually, in many things, Jesus was in substantial agreement with the leaders of the Jews, and particularly with the Pharisees. But in a lot of other ways, by the time of Jesus, the leaders of the Jews were missing the point of it all. And even before Jesus' time, the prophets decried the leaders of Israel, priests as well as kings, for not having the people's best interests at heart. So it's instructive to compare the leaders who were criticized by Jesus in today's Gospel reading, laying upon the people burdens too heavy to bear, making a public show of their piety, seeking privilege and prestige, coveting honor and renown, and perhaps, too, some leaders of the Christian congregation in Antioch who seemed to be headed the same way, with the behavior of the twelve priests in our reading from the book of Joshua, way back at the moment when the nation of Israel entered the promised land to reclaim it as the possession God had made their heritage many generations before. "So now," the Lord said to Joshua,

> "select twelve men from the tribes of Israel, one from each tribe. When the soles of the feet of the priests who bear the ark of the

"Muddy Feet"

Lord, the Lord of all the earth, rest in the waters of the Jordan, the waters of the Jordan flowing from above shall be cut off; they shall stand in a single heap."

When the people set out from their tents to cross over the Jordan, the priests bearing the ark of the covenant were in front of the people. Now the Jordan overflows all its banks throughout the time of harvest. So when those who bore the ark had come to the Jordan, and the feet of the priests bearing the ark were dipped in the edge of the water, the waters flowing from above stood still, rising up in a single heap . . . while those flowing toward the . . . Dead Sea, were wholly cut off. Then the people crossed over. . . . While all Israel were crossing over on dry ground, the priests who bore the ark of the covenant of the Lord stood on dry ground in the middle of the Jordan, until the entire nation finished crossing over the Jordan. (Josh 3:12–17, NRSV)

Just as important as *Moses* stretching out his arm and the waves parting so that the people could *escape slavery*, now the *priests* succeeded him by dipping their feet in the water of the Jordan and the river stopped flowing so that the people could *enter* the land of *hope and prosperity*. At certain times of the year, the Jordan is little more than a trickle, but in the springtime, as the rains fell upstream and the snows melted on the heights of Lebanon, the river would have been a torrent, quite as impassable as the Red Sea. How could the people enter the promised land in safety, except someone dare to act on the promise of God by venturing out into the threatening flood? But the twelve priests faithfully did just that, trusting in the purpose of God to *complete* the exodus from slavery, and *God* was faithful, too. Surely their feet got muddy, standing in the riverbed with the weight of God's law literally on their shoulders, but their concern for the well-being of the people they had been called to serve and their obedience to God was the thing that was needed for the people to cross on dry land and safe from harm into the future for which they had been waiting ever since the days of their ancestors Abraham and Sarah. And, at God's command, Joshua had twelve more men set up stones in the places where the priests stood, there in the middle of the riverbed, to commemorate the day, and the priests who bore the ark remained standing in the middle of the Jordan until everything was finished and all of the people had crossed over. Then Joshua commanded the priests, "'Come up out of the Jordan.' When the priests bearing the ark of the covenant of the Lord came up from the middle of the Jordan, and the soles of the priests' feet touched dry ground, the waters of the Jordan returned to their place and overflowed all its banks" (Josh 4:17–18, NRSV).

Thirty-first Sunday in Ordinary Time

The problem with the Pharisees and the scribes and the priests and the Sadducees of Jesus' day is that *they* weren't *about* to get *their* feet muddy. So pure were they in their own esteem that they wouldn't *think* of standing in the mud with people who were longing to cross over from the enslavement of illness, of poverty, of hunger, of homelessness, into the campground God had prepared for them on the other side of oppression and sin. Their own reputation in the eyes of the people around them, and in the eyes of God, was tied up with being *above* the real hurts and anxieties of common people, *above* the exigencies of poverty and sickness, *above* the temptations of circumstance and despair. And then came Jesus, who loved both God *and* sinners *so much* that he was willing to stand in the mud and hold back the flood of insult and ridicule and abuse and judgmentalism, and allow the lame and the hungry and the blind and the poor to camp and take rest on a little piece of the goodness that was God's promise to all of his people. It was in the waters of the same river Jordan where God intervened to work a mighty miracle of hope and freedom that Jesus was baptized, and the heavens themselves parted to allow the Spirit of God to descend and alight on him, and a voice from heaven announced God's pleasure with the one who now was anointed not to a pedestal high *above* the muck and the mire of human life, but to the very task of muddying his feet in people's problems, their sorrows and their sins, bearing the full weight of the law upon *his* shoulders, and opening up for them the way into the kingdom of heaven.

That is the way it is to be for Christian ministers, certainly for Christian pastors, but indeed for *everyone* who ministers, or serves, in the name of Jesus Christ. And *that* is supposed to be *all* of us, deputized to step into the waters that threaten to overwhelm folk whom God wants to lead out of bondage into freedom, out of darkness into light, out of despair into hope, out of sin into salvation. We can't do it from the safety, or the hygiene, of the shore. The evidence of our faithful service will likely include our muddy feet.

All Saints' Day

Spanish Springs Presbyterian Church, Sparks, Nevada

November 1, 2011

Revelation 7:9–17
1 John 3:1–3
Matthew 5:1–12

"The Inheritance"

About a week and a half ago, I participated in a panel discussion in a world religions class at Truckee Meadows Community College at the request of Rajan Zed, the class instructor. As many of you know, Raj is a Hindu, and is quite visibly active in the northern Nevada interfaith community. The subject of the discussion was reincarnation. When he first asked me to be one of the speakers for the class, I told him that I really would have nothing to contribute, since reincarnation is not a Christian belief. But he was insistent, as Raj can be, saying that, in that case, I should come and explain in twenty-five minutes why Christians *don't* believe in reincarnation. So, I finally relented, though I couldn't imagine how I would fill up twenty-five minutes.

The brief set of notes I made for myself started with how the Bible views history as linear, not cyclical—that God is at work within history bringing it from a beginning to a final completion, not simply consigning it to an endless repetition without any particular goal. And I made notes about how the resurrection is a promise of life after death, which means eternal life in the presence of God, not a promise that we will live life over again repeatedly in history and under essentially the same conditions and limitations that we are experiencing now. Though the vision of the heavenly city in our reading tonight from the Revelation of John is surely poetic, its promise is clear that "[t]hey will hunger no more, and thirst no more; the sun will not strike them, nor any scorching heat" (Rev 7:16, NRSV). And the *reason* for no more hunger and no more thirst and no more scorching heat isn't just because that's the way we would *like* it to be. The *reason*, John testifies, is that "the Lamb at the center of the throne will be their shepherd, and he will guide them to springs of the water of life, and God will wipe away every tear from their eyes" (Rev 7:17, NRSV). The vision of Revelation is all about the character and purpose of God.

Then, just three or four days before the class was to meet, Raj sent me a long list of references that he thought I should look up and respond to and he noted, by way of throwing down the reincarnation gauntlet, perhaps, that surveys indicate that a quarter of Americans, presumably including many people who identify themselves as Christians, believe in reincarnation. I haven't seen the questions involved in such surveys. I would be a little surprised if twenty-five percent of Americans actually *believe* in reincarnation, although I suppose I *wouldn't* be particularly surprised if twenty-five percent of Americans *wished* for reincarnation. The fear of death, and especially the fear that death is the end of everything so far as the individual is concerned, and the yearning for something other than the dark and the cold of the grave, are so great that a lot of people will grasp for *anything* as a possible alternative, even a repetition of their present earthly existence, complete with all its disappointments and pains.

But wishing for something, of course, even yearning for it, doesn't mean that it will happen. Thinking that something would be nice, right, or appropriate doesn't bring it about. And do-it-yourself religion, growing more and more popular in modern times, doesn't at all change the realities of death. Nor does the antiquity of traditional religions, such as Hinduism, that have for many centuries taught that we are born again, over and over—although, as I learned, in the case of Hinduism, each believer hopes ultimately to *break out* of the otherwise endless cycle of being born again and again into this same world of imperfections and sorrows.

"What about those passages in the Bible that speak of being born again?" Raj asked. "Doesn't that point to reincarnation?" Well, I explained, it isn't about coming again out of the womb as an infant—that was the very point at which Nicodemus the inquisitive Pharisee misapprehended what Jesus had told him. The whole discussion between Jesus and Nicodemus in the third chapter of John turns on that misunderstanding. "Then, what about those times that Jesus brought back to life someone who had died?" Well, I explained, the Bible indicates that Jesus brought Lazarus and Jairus's daughter back to life at the

"The Inheritance"

age at which they had *died*, not as *babies*, and they surely died *again*, eventually, hopefully at a ripe old age.

Fearful as the prospect of death might be for some people, and as good as life is for many, on balance, most men and women who have reached maturity generally realize that they have no reason to want to live it over again. They might like to have read some more books, visited some more places, spent more time with loved ones, achieved one more accomplishment in their occupation, but the prospect of an endless repetition of lifetimes as body-hopping spirits rather devalues the significance of *this* life, the way we have lived it, the relationships that we have had, the wisdom that we have acquired. Jesus certainly considered *this* life to be the one birth-to-death experience in which we can be faithful to God or not, can learn to love others or not, can become obedient disciples or not, can come to be saints or not—that is, inhabitants of the kingdom of God.

The very first time that Jesus taught in public, as Matthew tells the story, he began the lesson by explaining the realities and values and characteristics of the kingdom of heaven. Jesus spoke of things that many of his listeners were experiencing even then—poverty of spirit, grief, hunger and thirst, conflict, defamation, injustice, abuse—and he promised that, in the kingdom of heaven, there would be a reversal of all the present hurts and afflictions and disappointments and want. He spoke in terms of their being regarded as children of God, God's own heirs, inheriting the earth, holding title to the kingdom of heaven. And the key to all of this blessedness, the very condition and reason for it, was rooted in the faithfulness of God to the divine purpose of loving fellowship despite the sad circumstance, as the result of human sin, of imperfection in the world that God created as good. The hope of those who know their need is not to have a second or third or fourth experience of all life's difficulties, but to know that beyond the unfairness and disappointments and pain of the world there is an eternity of plenty and peace and justice, and that all those who humbly recognize their dependence on God and are grateful for God's gracious care are heirs to all the blessings that God has to offer, which are considerable, and which are inevitable, and which cannot be taken away from those who love God and trust God and seek above all else to please God, their heavenly parent. So even though and because they do not return evil for evil in their own defense but trust God to vindicate them, even though and because they are weighed down by the sins of the world and by the sorrow of loss, even though and because they are humble and gentle in spirit rather than assertive and insistent upon their rights, the kingdom will be theirs, they will be comforted, they will have a full share of the creation renewed—and so they are blessed even now, while all these things are yet to be. Even though and because they feel an emptiness when they consider their own sinfulness and survey the sinfulness around them, even though and because they freely forgive those who do them wrong, even though and because they are not persuaded to disobedience by the world's seductions and allurements, they will be filled to overflowing and will be forgiven all their own sins and will be privileged to experience what was denied even the great figures of the Bible—they will be rewarded by being permitted to look into the face of God. Even though and because they have risked their own comfort by working to reconcile those who are estranged and hostile, even though and because they have been insulted and tormented for trying to be faithful to God, even though and because they have been defamed and lied about because of their beliefs, they will be recognized as God's own children—which means heirs to all that God has to give, a reward beyond calculation in the kingdom that has already dawned with the coming of Christ and will finally be seen in its fullness when Christ comes again and declares history closed and completed. "Beloved," 1 John assures believers, "we are God's children now" (1 John 3:2a, NRSV). We are *already* the designated heirs. We are *already* saints, destined to walk freely into the city up to the throne and before the Lamb to declare in voices of the purest praise, "Salvation belongs to our God who is seated on the throne, and to the Lamb" (Rev 7:10b, NRSV)!

The world is what it is. Poverty, bereavement, hunger and thirst, war, persecution—we can't expect better when people disobey God by living selfishly, acting indulgently, grasping greedily, taking pleasure at inflicting hurt. Far better than *repeating* history, far better than living our lives over and over again, is the promise of the kingdom of God. Far better than the popular wish for reincarnation is the faithful hope, sealed in the resurrection of Jesus Christ, that God will not just birth us again into the world to see how we do the *next* time, see whether it's any better for us on the *second* go-around, or the *third*, or the *fourth*, but to know and act upon the testimony of scripture that God acknowledges us as sons and daughters, and therefore as heirs of heaven. *Already* we are within God's embrace. *Already* we are God's children, even in the midst of our yearnings and our prayers and our questions and our sufferings. *Already* the blessings are ours, if we hear and believe and accept and act upon God's choice of comfort over bereavement, of humility over presumption, of sharing over hoarding, of mercy over vengeance, of reconciliation over conflict. Is it any kind of blessing to have a *second* lifetime in which we might possibly acquire more wealth or claim more respect, in which we might suffer less hardship or endure less discord? Or is the blessing in knowing now, in *this* lifetime, that God's purpose is not lost among all the real and present hurts and inequalities, but is testified to as true and inevitable every time someone turns to God in hope and trust, and every time someone gives up riches and

"The Inheritance"

advantage to share with someone who has less, and every time someone risks his or her own wealth and reputation and physical well-being in order to bring an end to alienation and disharmony?

This day is an important one on the church's calendar. It originated with the early church's recognition that it is right to remember the faithful who have gone before us, who have lived and died trusting in God and professing faith in Jesus Christ, both those whose names and deeds are well-known and those whose names and deeds are known only to God, and who now inhabit heaven, where they sing praise forever before the throne of God and of the Lamb. But it is not just an occasion for remembering the faithful of the past. We observe All Saints' Day mindful that we *ourselves* have been adopted by God, and have been made heirs to the things of heaven. We have been promised not a repetition of life in the world as it has always been, but everlasting citizenship in a world redeemed and renewed. Greed and pride and fear and strife still assert themselves in this life. But their power has been broken. It is overcome by the sacrificial death of God's own Son who himself recognized and gave thanks that God supplied his need, who himself mourned the sins of the world, who himself forgave freely, and who himself, when he met with rejection and injustice, went humbly to the cross, laying down his life to reconcile us to God and reconcile us to each other. So *we* look for the *resurrection* of the dead and the life of the world to *come*.

THIRTY-SECOND SUNDAY IN ORDINARY TIME

First Presbyterian Church, Dodge City, Kansas

NOVEMBER 10, 1996

Joshua 24:1–3a, 14–25
1 Thessalonians 14:13–18
Matthew 25:1–13

"Prepared for the Best"

The musical "Fiddler on the Roof" is filled with memorable scenes. One which is a favorite with many people, no doubt in part because of the poignant song "Sunrise, Sunset," is the wedding of the milkman Rep Tevye's oldest daughter to Motl the poor tailor. For a lot of us non-Jews, that scene was an introduction to traditional Jewish marriage customs—including the evening candlelight parade from the groom's house to the home of the bride, and then on to the place of the ceremony, held under a canopy. Doing everything just so is a solemn responsibility, but the event itself is joyful beyond words. And there is great expectancy surrounding it all. The entire community is involved. Everybody wants to have a part in blessing the couple as they begin their life together—children, elders, and all the people in between. The celebration does not belong simply to the bride and groom. It is an opportunity for everyone to depart from the daily routine to have a party, to reunite with relatives, to renew acquaintances, to indulge in rich food, to be liberal with wine, to joke, to dance, to recall the joy of their own wedding. The scene makes us wistful for a less sophisticated life. A lot of those pleasures get lost in all of our modern wedding rituals—printed invitations and picture-taking and the arrange-

"Prepared for the Best"

ments for caterers and florists and bridesmaids' dresses and tuxedos and all the rest—but, even without the hand-held candles and the procession and the canopy, most of us know about the joy of a wedding, and how everyone wants the celebration to be just right—how we want for the bride and groom to have a wonderfully memorable day, and for all the guests to enjoy fine hospitality.

Whether a Jewish wedding under a canopy or a Christian wedding in a sanctuary, the rush of last-minute preparations means that the wedding does not always start precisely on schedule. I have noticed, as a minister, that the wedding *rehearsal* never starts on time. In ancient times, when people did not have wristwatches or indeed any time piece more accurate than a sundial, precise timing of such events was not possible. Nor was it important, really—the whole community was involved in the preparations, and the entire day would have been given over to getting ready. At the wedding itself, everyone was there for the *celebration*, not just fitting it in between other activities. It was more important than any *other* business could be. Knowing that there might be any number of reasons that things would not start quite on time, the people who had official roles to play in the wedding festivities would want to be prepared to perform their duties whenever they might be called upon.

Jesus told a story to his disciples about a group of bridesmaids who were supposed to go to meet the bridegroom, probably to accompany him from his house to fetch his bride and take her, seated in a litter, to the wedding ceremony, where they would exchange their vows. The wedding custom included carrying lamps or, more likely, torches, to light the groom's way in the evening darkness—the Greek word that is here rendered as "lamps" in most versions is translated as "torches" in other parts of the Bible. The bridesmaids had their lamps or torches with them, but, when they arrived at the home of the groom, he wasn't there, or wasn't yet ready, and they fell asleep while they were waiting for him. By and by, the maidens were awakened with shouts that the bridegroom was finally on his way, but some of them had neglected to bring enough oil to keep their lights burning through the delayed ceremony.

While these bridesmaids who had not been prepared for the delay were out trying to find a 7-Eleven that carried lamp oil, the others who had the foresight to bring extra oil *with* them got to *perform their* role and take part in all the festivities. By the time the foolish maidens finally returned from their errand, the vows had been said. The feasting had begun. The doors of the banquet hall were shut. Not only had the foolish maidens failed in their duty. They missed out on all the fun. And the simple reason was that they had not planned ahead to be prepared whenever the wedding might start. The social event of the season had passed them by—probably the best party that had happened in that community in a long time. Jesus told his disciples that the kingdom of heaven would be like that situation. Some people would be ready for it, and others would not. Would his *disciples* be prepared for the kingdom when it comes? Were they thinking beyond the immediate present and their own welfare, the routine tasks and daily distractions? Were they preparing themselves to be ready for the party *whenever* it might begin?

When we hear the scripture stories about readiness, we perhaps think in terms of being ready for the coming of the Lord by being sinless, so that we do not fall into eternal misery at the second coming. There are many places in scripture where Jesus warns people to repent. But Jesus did not introduce this parable by saying that it tells what *hell* will be like—Jesus did not use this occasion to teach his disciples to be prepared for the *worst*. Jesus introduced *this* parable by saying that it tells what the kingdom of *heaven* will be like—he was urging his disciples to be prepared for the *best*. He did not want his followers to miss out on the joy of the kingdom, which might come to fullness at any moment. "Look!" shouted someone after the maidens had fallen asleep. "Here is the bridegroom! Come out to meet him" (Matt 25:6b, NRSV). That was not a cry of *fear*, but a shout of *joy*. Their oil had burned low in waiting for him. Fortunately, some—the wise ones who were prepared for the contingency of delay—had an extra supply, so that they were able to fulfill their role dutifully, and they ended up at the banquet. Unfortunately, others—the foolish ones who never considered that they might be waiting all evening—awoke to find their flames burning low, and they had no oil with which to revive them. The party rolled on without them.

Matthew's original audience was a first-century church, probably in Syria, that was enduring harsh persecution and was surely wondering why Jesus had not yet returned as he had promised. It must have been difficult to continue day in and day out, doing one's Christian duty of caring for others, loving others, forgiving others, sacrificing for others, while living under constant threat of being disowned by family and shunned by friends and ridiculed by strangers and arrested by authorities. How could believers keep their gaze on the treasures of *heaven* while fearing *earthly woe*? How could they nurture a sense of blessing in the midst of hardship? How could they maintain an attitude of thanksgiving in an atmosphere of harassment? How could they stay joyfully alert to opportunities of giving witness to their faith while suffering oppression? Surely they were experiencing the worst! The *gospel* testified that their *Lord* wanted them to prepare for the *best*.

We people of modern Western culture have a hard time identifying with the fears and the hardships of the early Christians. We are not persecuted for our faith, most of us; we can hardly conceive of what faithful Christians in countries that are hostile to the church must endure on a regular basis. Indeed,

"Prepared for the Best"

in our culture of temporary loyalties and convenient allegiances, of immediate gratification and affluent ease, some of us find unimaginable surrendering up one's life rather than surrendering up a copy of the scriptures, of saying goodbye to one's friends and one's fortune rather than recanting one's faith. It's not that we aren't prepared for the *worst*—we are probably the most insured people on the face of the earth, insured against catastrophes of all sorts. We prepare ourselves for medical bills, for crop failures, for disability, for theft, for fire, for accident, for malpractice claims. We may, some of us, even think of our *Christianity* as insurance against *hell*. But a lot of us, including many of us in the church, are not ready to respond joyfully when the kingdom of heaven dawns upon us, either at the return of Christ, or in the daily calls to discipleship that God brings our way. We are dominated in thought and calendar by the demands of job, of school, of family, sometimes even by the busy-ness of the church. We are so occupied with protecting ourselves against financial troubles, against poor grades, against almost every earthly contingency, that it's a real question whether we would even *hear* the joyful shout, "Look! Here is the bridegroom! Come out to meet him!" (Matt 25:6b, NRSV)—"Look! The kingdom of heaven is open before you! Come step through the door!" We are so busy, many of us, with the anxieties of schedule and success that opportunities to light the Lord's way by pausing to feed the hungry, or welcome the stranger, or clothe the naked, or visit the prisoner, go unheeded. Even a word of cheer often goes unspoken, a compassionate embrace goes ungiven, a sacrificial deed goes undone. We have not thought it was our job to be peacemakers. Someone else can look to comforting the sorrowful. I have to think first about me and mine—so we convince ourselves. We haven't been prepared in spirit; in our rush to measurable result and visible achievement that will win the world's approval and financial reward, the oil of humility and mercy and generosity can run low without our even noticing. The opportunity to answer someone's need with faithful ministry is fleeting. We miss the summons. We miss the joy. We miss the best. We miss the kingdom of heaven.

"Blessed are the poor in spirit" (Matt 5:3a, NRSV), said Jesus—the ones who know that they can't buy eternal life, can't earn salvation, the ones who are despised by the world, but who are content to receive the gift of God's grace daily, thankfully, joyfully, who look only to *God* for *their* satisfaction, and who give freely of themselves to others as God has given freely to them—blessed are they, "for theirs is the kingdom of heaven" (Matt 5:3b, NRSV). Theirs is the best. Having no protection of their own against the abuse of others, making no claim to be able to save themselves, such people live in daily trust only upon God. Their joy is not in paid-up insurance policies and pantries full to bursting and admission to the best schools and access to the most prestigious social circles, but in a manner of kindness and a habit of generosity. They take *their* fulfillment not behind walls built thick and high to shut out the cold blast of human cruelty and indifference, but in a vulnerable alertness to *serve* others and a quick eagerness to *forgive* others. The torches with which *they* light the way of the Lord Jesus Christ are well-oiled with deeds of mercy and acts of love in obedience to the Great Commandment, and they patiently but expectantly await the final consummation by living out what they profess—love of God and love of neighbor, offering themselves as ready comforters, healers and reconcilers. They are not oblivious to pain and sorrow, to temptation and doubt. They have discovered that the midnights of life are in fact the very times when God may find us most receptive to heaven's highest joys, *if* we are prepared to respond to them.

Almost from infancy, we are taught to be prepared for the worst. But Jesus Christ wants *his* followers to be prepared for the *best*. While we wait for the coming of the kingdom of heaven, our attention may drift, we may give heed to the voices of greed, pride, self-pity, and self-love, and begin to mistake *them* for wisdom, and waste our time and our ability and our money in ways that do nothing to light the way of Christ to the joyful banquet hall. But the truly *wise persist*, even through long delay in Christ's final coming, in faithful recognition that the kingdom of heaven may open to us at any moment. In fact, the kingdom of heaven comes near to us very often, sometimes in the form of opportunity to join Jesus Christ in selfless ministry, shining God's grace into every dark place *out there*, sometimes in the presence of Jesus Christ himself, shining God's grace into every dark place *in here*. The opportunities to join with our Lord in the joyful life of the kingdom are right in front of us, if we are alert to the summons and if we are ready to respond. Let not the emergency of gladness catch us off-guard and find us unprepared. "[A]t midnight, there was a shout, 'Look! Here is the bridegroom! Come out to meet him'" (Matt 25:6, NRSV). As individuals, as a church, are *we* prepared for the *best*?

Thirty-third Sunday in Ordinary Time

Spanish Springs Presbyterian Church, Sparks, Nevada

November 16, 2008

Judges 4:1–7
1 Thessalonians 5:1–11
Matthew 25:14–30

"It's Not About Us"

In that wonderful motion picture, *The African Queen*, Charlie Allnut, played by Humphrey Bogart, suffers several deprivations at the insistence of Rose Sayer, an imperious moralist played by Kathryn Hepburn. After she dumps all of his stock of gin in the river, following a drinking binge, he asks, "What you being so mean for, Miss? A man takes a drop too much once in a while. It's only human nature," to which Rose, the straight-laced sister of an African missionary, replies, "Nature, Mr. Allnut, is what we are put in this world to rise above."[1]

Fortunately, most of us have a more positive appraisal of nature as something that is within the orbit of God's providence and purpose. So most of us are able to acknowledge that the natural order is basically *good*. And yet it is undeniable that there is a "law of the jungle" at work in nature that is not particularly Christ-like. The prophet Isaiah pictures the scene when God's purpose for all creation is finally fulfilled: the wolf shall live with the lamb, the leopard will lie down with the young goat, the lion will be a vegetarian,

---

1. Huston, *African Queen*.

and even a baby will be able to play alongside venomous snakes without being harmed. But nature as we know it is still far from that day: wolves devour sheep, leopards prey on livestock, the lion is a feared aggressor, and parents could be arrested for knowingly setting their child in an adder's den. And the human creature, left to its own inclinations, tends to be self-centered to the point of being willing to harm other parts of creation or at least failing to come to their aid.

Frankly, we are born not *generous* but *greedy*, not near so interested in giving as in taking, concerned primarily to satisfy our own desires rather than the needs of others. Enlightened self-interest may prompt us to curb some of these characteristics in a society in which the desires of millions of people are in competition, but raw nature teaches us mainly to be cautious and selfish, because the natural instincts are all about self-preservation and self-satisfaction. That is why we so quickly go to war. That is why some people live in mansions while others live in abandoned cars. That is why politicians win votes when they appeal to the voters' pocketbooks.

As a child of the fifties and sixties, I am dismayed that war is still such an easy option for our nation, that a larger percentage of people live in poverty today than half a century ago, and that appealing to greed is still the most effective political advertising. There were appallingly few "Ask not what your country can do for you" moments from either party in the recent political campaign. What has happened to the generation that sang and marched to change all that?

Even before Abraham set off on his journey to the land God would show him, God told him that the purpose of it all was so that he and his family would be a blessing to others. Even before the liberated Hebrew slaves entered the promised land, God instructed them through Moses that they were to make an offering to God of the firstfruits of the land they were going into. The very first crop was to be a gift to *God*, which meant that *most* of it would end up being given to the *poor*. The people of God could not even recoup their original investment, setting enough grain aside as seed for the *next* planting, until *after* they had given the *first* part of the harvest to *God*. That of course meant that these nomadic people who had never farmed before had to *plant* the *original* seed, trusting that it would grow, rather than *eating* it, taking advantage of the bird in the hand, so to speak. Wolves and leopards and lions and snakes don't know anything about investing, or planting. It's not a natural instinct. But, from the beginning of their time in the land that God had given them, the Israelites were going to have to invest, to plant, and therefore to trust the outcome to God. And the purpose for that, of course, was that their prime concern would never be *themselves*. They must learn to trust *God* from day to

"It's Not About Us"

day. The fruits of their labor would be offered to God for the benefit of *others*, and so would be a *blessing* to others.

Virtually any place you look in the Bible specifies or implies that the things God puts at our disposal are to be used for a greater purpose than just meeting our own desires and providing for our own comfort. Regrettably, that is not the message that a lot of people walk away from churches with on Sunday mornings. And, frankly, the modern phenomenon of *marketing* churches, and the appalling development of marketing *Jesus*, has led a lot of people to conclude that the Christian faith is ultimately all about *me*—my getting to heaven in the *end*, my getting the good things out of life *now*. "Come and join us in making an offering to God," "Come and join us in pouring ourselves out for others"—when was the last time you saw a church advertise itself *that* way? But if anything is clear from an honest reading of the Bible, it is that God's purpose is to bring us out of ourselves, to prompt us to make an offering of our life to God, to receive what God has given us not as an *entitlement* but as a *trust*, and to invest it on behalf of God's purpose of bringing good news to the poor, of proclaiming release to the captives and recovery of sight to the blind, of letting the oppressed go free, and of proclaiming the year of the Lord's favor—the things that *Jesus* was about and that he taught his *disciples* to be about.

The Bible is not about me; it is about God at work in Jesus Christ to bring about God's redemptive purpose for all humankind, indeed, all creation. The gospel is not about satisfying my desires; it is about the sacrifice that God was willing to make on my behalf to free me and all people from my, their, our, self-centeredness, which is really idolatry, and which is what leads to greed and hatred and lust and covetousness and all the rest of the things that scripture says we are supposed to overcome, by the power of the Holy Spirit at work within us. Worship is not about my entertainment; it is about my giving to God what God deserves. Christianity is not for the purpose of nourishing what is popularly referred to as human nature, but about calling us to a higher plane of intention and behavior—one that fundamentally reorients us away from a focus on ourselves and toward the well-being of others. And that means a radical reorientation from acquiring and accumulating to nurturing and giving away.

Jesus told a parable about the end of the age: "For it is as if a man, going on a journey, summoned his slaves and entrusted his property to them" (Matt 25:14, NRSV). And we recall that he gave five talents to one slave, two talents to another, and but a single talent to a third. The one who received the five talents used them to produce five talents more; the one who received the two talents used them to produce two talents more. Both amounts were huge sums of money—a single talent was many times more than what the average person

Thirty-third Sunday in Ordinary Time

could earn in a year, so investing the money constituted a considerable risk. The *third* slave, to whom only a *single* talent had been entrusted, simply *sat* on it, satisfied with the knowledge that if it wasn't *spent*, it wouldn't be *lost*. When he returned from his journey, the man was impressed with the profit that his slaves had made who had taken the risk of investing what he had put in their hands, but he harshly condemned the one who had taken no risk at all and therefore had nothing to return to him but the original amount. In fact, his master called that slave *worthless*, for he had not accomplished *anything*. Why did he think the master had given him the talent in the *first* place? It wasn't about *him*. It was about achieving something worthwhile for the master's account; it was about investing what had been entrusted to the slave so that there might be the possibility of a return on the money; it was about trusting the master's wisdom in placing the money into the slave's hands so that it could be invested and given a chance to be productive.

I don't know whether anyone in our congregation rationalizes not making a pledge of the firstfruits of his or her labor on the grounds that it might be too risky an investment. But I do know that making an offering to God by way of pledging the first part of our income, and doing so generously and joyfully and thankfully, fulfills *today* what Moses declared that God deserves from all his people who are grateful for what God has placed in their hands. And I also know that holding *on* to what God has placed in our hands, *not* investing it in the work of Jesus Christ through his church, is to invite the same appraisal that the master laid on the servant who took the coin and kept it and, on the day of accounting, had nothing to show for the trust that God had placed in him. And I suspect that it is the result of a misunderstanding of what the Christian faith is ultimately all about, what Christian worship is ultimately all about, what the Christian church is ultimately all about—not to get us into heaven, not to get us through the week, not to get us into a group of people who can't reject us but have to put up with us no matter how selfish we are. Faith, worship, church—ultimately, it's not really about *us*. It's about *God*, and gratitude for what God has *done* for us and is *doing* for us, especially in the sacrificial gift of Jesus Christ. Is the God who created the world and the whole universe worthy of our praise? Is the God who gave us life and breath and sustains us all our days worthy of our offering? Is the God who makes it possible for us to have food on our table and a roof over our head and who surrounds us with family and friends and the company of the saints worthy of our pledge to put God at the top of our priority list for giving, spending, investing what he has graciously entrusted to us?

The slaves to whom the master entrusted his money should have felt flattered and privileged that their master had such a high opinion of their ability to accomplish his purpose. The one who *hid* the talent and did *not* invest it in essence was *disputing* the master's *judgment,* *denying* the master's *wisdom,* showing *ingratitude* for the master's *trust.* Angry, the master took away the one talent he handed back to him and gave it to the slave who had taken the greatest risk and, so, had made the greatest return on his investment. The slave with the one talent explained that he had feared he would be punished for investing if the money didn't return a profit. And so he had failed to part with it, but kept it, held on to it, decided to preserve it safe for the unknowns of what the economy might be like tomorrow, what the household needs might be in the future, what better opportunities there might be down the road. It's funny how all those uncertainties and contingencies can paralyze us into what is finally indistinguishable from greed and distrust and ingratitude. And then God gets nothing from us except maybe our leftovers. That's not faithfulness. "Oh, but the wise person, the prudent person, the cautious person who wants to be sure to have enough holds on to what he or she has." After all, we say, it's human nature to be concerned for our own well-being. Maybe. But, you see, it's not really about *us.*

Christ the King
Spanish Springs Presbyterian Church, Sparks, Nevada
November 21, 1999

Ezekiel 34:11–16, 20–24
Ephesians 1:15–23
Matthew 25:31–46

"Faces of the King"

The people of the kingdom were greatly excited. Their beloved king, known far and wide for being generous and kind to all of his subjects and concerned for their welfare, had announced the first annual good citizenship award ceremony. Although no prize had yet been announced, it seemed certain that such an important award would be accompanied by a prize of great expense and prestige—speculation centered on a new luxury automobile and dinner with the king in the palace. Of course, many people were calculating how they could win the award, although no criteria had been specified. To their credit, not a single person in the kingdom sought the award merely for the sake of the anticipated *prize*, although of course that was an added incentive. The greater motive was to show how much they loved their king, how much they appreciated his generosity and kindness.

The most prominent citizen of the kingdom was a man named Humphrey J. Limpet. So well-known was he, in fact, that it would have been something of an embarrassment if he were not to receive the award. When he heard about it, he entered into the spirit of the contest with characteristic zeal. Mr. Limpet was a great planner—he was quite good at organizing his own life and the life

"Faces of the King"

of his family and the life of anyone else who sought his advice and counsel. So the first thing he did was to decide upon a plan. First, he would announce the formation of a Citizens' Kingdom Improvement Committee with himself as chairperson and twelve other prominent citizens as committee members. The committee would have the task of conducting a study of all the citizens of the kingdom and making suggestions about how they could improve the quality of the moral and social life of the kingdom. Mr. Limpet was painfully aware that some of his fellow citizens were not showing adequate respect toward their king who had been so generous and kind to his subjects; some people did not keep their homes and shops neat and clean, some did not dress properly as befits people with pride in their appearance, some did not behave according to the standards of rule and custom for the kingdom; why, some more recent arrivals among the citizenry did not even speak the official language! Mr. Limpet himself had always tried to set a good example by keeping his place of business tidy, the grounds of his home neat, and himself well-groomed. He went out of his way to observe the rules that the king had established and to follow the customs of the kingdom. But as for many of his fellow citizens, there was certainly much room for improvement. Surely the king would be grateful for any assistance in bringing order and maintaining the standards of hygiene in his realm.

The second part of Mr. Limpet's plan was to conduct a personal speaking tour throughout the kingdom in praise of the king, drawing to the attention of any neglectful subject the appropriate way of showing suitable homage to their monarch who was so generous and kind. Difficult as it was for Mr. Limpet to understand how some people could be so disrespectful, he was aware that a regrettably large proportion of citizens simply did not attend the weekly celebration held in the king's honor just outside the palace. He himself had *always* participated, and had not the least idea why everyone did not. Nor could he understand how anyone might fail to speak highly of such a generous and kind king at every opportunity, just as he did. Mr. Limpet was convinced that he was providing an indispensable service for his fellow citizens as well as for the king by addressing the issue.

It so happened that the day on which Mr. Limpet devised his plan was the day before the weekly celebration in front of the palace. He hit upon the happy idea of announcing the formation of the Citizens' Kingdom Improvement Committee and his speaking tour the very next day, at the celebration. What better way to demonstrate his genuine devotion to the king? As he fell asleep that night, Mr. Limpet was even entertaining the possibility that his announcement would discourage anyone *else* from even *attempting* to win the first annual good citizenship award.

Christ the King

Mr. Limpet awoke the next morning and dressed with extra thoughtfulness to detail; he would want to look his very best if he were going to be the center of attention at the celebration. He took his appointment book from his pocket and checked it again, to be sure that he wasn't forgetting anything. The celebration, as usual, would be at ten-thirty in the morning. On his way to the celebration, he would mail the invitations to the twelve prominent people whom he desired to serve with him on the Citizens' Kingdom Improvement Committee. After the celebration, he would drive to the airport to catch his flight to his first speaking engagement, stopping off at the police station on the way to inform the police commissioner of his absence from home for a few days and asking whether it could be patrolled extra carefully while he was away.

As Mr. Limpet started to back out of his driveway, he saw, in the rearview mirror, a poorly-dressed woman sitting on the sidewalk, one hand clutching her stomach and the other outstretched to passers-by who were likewise on their way to the weekly celebration. He honked his horn so that she would move out of the way of his car, but she did not budge. "Bother!" he thought, as he stopped the car and got out. "I'm going to be late!"

"See here, madam, I'm afraid that you'll have to move out of the way of my car."

She turned a care-worn face up toward him and stared for a few seconds.

"I must get to the celebration, of course!"

The woman nodded slowly and shifted to a place beside the driveway. As Mr. Limpet hustled back to his automobile, he thought about the missed opportunity of telling the vagrant that *she* really ought to be at the celebration, too, but in the interest of time, he did not attempt to correct his oversight. Besides, she was hardly dressed suitably for the celebration. Driving down the street, he glanced in the rearview mirror and saw that a teenaged girl carrying a grocery bag had stopped beside the woman, and seemed to be handing the bag to her. "Hmm," Mr. Limpet said to himself, "that girl looks like Evie Cochrane," but in his preoccupation with his task, he thought nothing more about the incident.

After parking his car, Mr. Limpet got out and deposited the invitations in a nearby mailbox, then walked briskly toward the palace, where people were already gathering for the celebration. It was a warm day, and folks were lining up at the refreshment booths for soft drinks to combat the heat. Mr. Limpet would have liked a cool drink himself, but of course he was in need of getting to the speaker's platform, so he did not indulge in such a pleasure. As he neared the palace, he passed an old man seated on a bench, his face dripping with perspiration, rather shabbily dressed and showing no sign of expecting to participate in the celebration. "A disgusting way to come to the palace grounds!" thought Mr. Limpet as he surveyed the crowd.

He pressed on toward the platform. "Fellow subjects of our generous and kind king," said Mr. Limpet, "I appear before you at this glorious celebration to announce the organization of a Citizens' Kingdom Improvement Committee of twelve prominent citizens and myself who will make suggestions how the quality of the moral and social life of the kingdom can be improved. I am sure you are aware that some of our fellow citizens are not showing adequate respect toward the king who has been so generous and kind; some people do not keep their homes and shops neat and clean, some do not dress properly, some do not behave according to the standards of rule and custom for the kingdom, why, some among us do not even speak the official language! Surely our king deserves better."

As he said this, his eye caught a glimpse of the man on the bench. Barney Spencer was handing him a soft drink obviously purchased from the refreshment stand, as Linda Parker walked toward him from the souvenir shop, carrying a brightly-colored shirt and what looked like flowered Bermuda shorts. The sight of such attire was almost enough to cause Mr. Limpet to lose his concentration.

"Furthermore," he continued, "I want you all to know that I am leaving immediately for the airport, where I will depart on a speaking tour in praise of our king, drawing to the attention of any neglectful subject the appropriate way of showing suitable homage to our monarch who is so generous and kind."

Everyone applauded with great enthusiasm, and Mr. Limpet smiled and waved to the crowd. He pushed his way through the throng of people back toward where he had parked his automobile. "Tsk, tsk," he said under his breath, shaking his head as he passed the man on the bench, now smiling and adorned in the brightly-colored shirt and flowered Bermuda shorts, sipping on a glass of lemonade.

He was surprised, when he got to his car, to discover leaning against his right front fender a young man, rather pale-looking and shivering, in spite of the heat. As Mr. Limpet approached, the young man turned his face toward him, and Mr. Limpet could see that his eyes were glassy. "Poor fellow," thought Mr. Limpet to himself, "but why did he have to choose *my* car to lean against?"

"I'm sorry, my good man," said Mr. Limpet, "but I'm afraid I must have the use of my automobile."

The young man nodded rather absent-mindedly, and with great effort pushed himself away from the fender and staggered toward the curb, where he sat down.

Christ the King

"Thank you; I'm sorry to have had to bother you," said Mr. Limpet, not without a note of genuine concern in his voice.

"Are you alright?" asked Winnie Smith as she got out of the car parked next to Mr. Limpet's, and bent over the pale young man.

Mr. Limpet got in his car and looked at his watch. "Still time to swing by the police station on my way to the airport," he thought to himself.

"Thank you," said Mr. Limpet to the police officer who opened the door for him at the police station. "May I see the police commissioner?" he asked of the desk sergeant.

"He's not in his office right now," the desk sergeant replied. "Can I help you, Mr. Limpet?"

"Yes," said Mr. Limpet, glancing at his watch. "I am leaving on a very important speaking tour to draw the attention of our people to the appropriate way to show homage to our king, and wondered whether there could be an extra patrol around my house each day while I am gone."

"Certainly," replied the desk sergeant, "especially since you are going to perform such an important public service. You might almost ought to start over there," he said, nodding toward the iron bars across the room. A pathetic and frightened-looking man peered out of the corner of his cell at Mr. Limpet. "Caught him just this morning breaching the rules of the kingdom."

"Why do people do such things?" asked Mr. Limpet, not really expecting an answer.

"You could *ask* him," replied the desk sergeant with a shrug, "but he wouldn't understand you—doesn't even speak our language."

Mr. Limpet looked at the desk sergeant with an expression of perplexity, and then back toward the man in the cell, whose face, he now noticed, was of a different complexion than his own.

Another man had come into the police station now, Tom Murphy, a fellow who never seemed to care about his own appearance, and he asked the desk sergeant, "Do you have any prisoners today that I may visit?"

"Over there," the desk sergeant pointed without looking up from his work, "but you're wasting your time."

"It's not a waste," said Tom, walking toward the cell.

Suddenly remembering his more pressing concern, Mr. Limpet turned toward the door.

Mr. Limpet came to the weekly celebration a little earlier than usual, in spite of the fact that he was tired, having just arrived back home from his speaking tour the night before. He certainly did not want to risk being late on the very day that the first annual good citizenship award was announced. He was a little disappointed not to see a new luxury automobile or any other

"Faces of the King"

obvious prize on display in front of the palace, but consoled himself with the thought that the award might bring with it instead a prize trip around the world, perhaps even one on which he could serve as a sort of special good will ambassador, speaking in many different countries in praise of the king's generosity and kindness.

The crowd gathered in front of the palace gates, but 10:30 came and went, without any sight of the king. 10:40. 10:50. 11:00. Mr. Limpet grew impatient, as did the other people gathered around. Just then, people behind him started cheering, and the crowd parted as the king walked toward the platform, not from the direction of the *palace*, but from the *city*. The king mounted the platform.

"As you know," he said, "I am here to announce the winner of the first annual good citizenship award. Actually, there has been a tie."

Mr. Limpet's countenance fell noticeably.

"A tie between Evie Cochrane, Barney Spencer, Linda Parker, Winnie Smith, and Tom Murphy."

One by one, the people named came forward, hesitantly, it seemed, and somewhat confused. Miss Cochrane shook her head in dismay. Mr. Murphy said, "You don't mean *me*, do you?" But the king nodded. Mrs. Smith blushed.

Mr. Limpet was astounded and deeply hurt, but also curious. "Why *them* and not *me*?" he wondered.

"To you five," said the king, "I give my kingdom. From this time forth, all that is mine is yours."

"But your highness—" protested Evie.

"Why, what have *I* done to deserve *this*?" asked Barney.

"There must be some mistake," said Linda.

"Do you have the right Winnie Smith?" asked Winnie.

Tom just stood there looking dumbfounded.

"Come, inherit my kingdom, for I was hungry and you gave me food, I was thirsty and you gave me something to drink, I was a stranger and you welcomed me, I was naked and you gave me clothing, I was sick and you took care of me."

"But when—?" they started, but the king held up his hand to silence their question.

"Your highness!" shouted Mr. Limpet, in spite of his reverence for the king. "Have you perhaps not heard what *I* have been doing?"

"I am aware," answered the king. "I am aware."

He looked out over the people gathered in front of the palace. "As a good king, I must watch over all my people, must care for all my people, must be in sympathy with all my people, must identify with all my people. I *live* for my *people*, and I live *through* my people. I see myself in each of your faces; your smiles are my joy, your tears are my sorrow, your human kindness is my love, your anguish is my pain. You all saw my face this week—the face of the hungry, the face of the thirsty, the face of the stranger, the face of the naked, the face of the sick, the face of the imprisoned."

Suddenly, Mr. Limpet remembered the occasions on which he had recently seen Evie and Barney and Linda and Winnie and Tom.

"You mean that *you*—?" Mr. Limpet started to ask the king, but then broke off the question, embarrassed and not knowing what to say.

"You mean that *you*—?" asked Tom Murphy, as the king embraced the five surprised good citizens and led them into the palace.

Thanksgiving

Spanish Springs Presbyterian Church, Sparks, Nevada
November 27, 2002

Deuteronomy 8:1–10
Philippians 4:6–20
Matthew 6:25–33

"The Good Thing About Hunger"

Christmas morning. Presents under the tree. Children up at 5:00 a.m. Parents pulled out of bed. Children highly focused, like lions ready to pounce on prey. Was that a starter's pistol? Children dive into the pile of gifts, and each picks one up, rips off wrapping paper, glances at the contents, tosses it aside, and grabs for another. A few minutes later, torn gift wrap is everywhere, presents cluttering the floor. Then the question "Is that all there is?" Depression.

All of us have experienced such Christmas mornings, I think. Though the scenario may seem somewhat exaggerated, we can probably all identify with it to some degree, either remembering our own childhood, or our own parenthood, or remembering our dismay when we were visiting relatives or friends for Christmas. I have recently been taping episodes of "Little House on the Prairie" for Beth to watch from time to time. Each season that the show ran, I think, there was a Christmas episode, and every Christmas, the children's presents consisted of a homemade toy, like a rocking horse or a wagon, and a pair of socks or mittens, if the farm had been good to them that year, and perhaps some nuts, and an orange, and a stick of peppermint, and maybe a penny, and the children were so pleased. Seeing the contrast between Christmas then and Christmas now makes us laugh. And then it makes us cry.

A lot of homes in our country, even a lot of middle-class homes, will probably have fewer presents under the Christmas tree this year than last year, and, for many of us, last year's Christmas gifts were more modest than the year before. The stock market boom of the nineties, and the technology boom that fueled it, took the economy to giddy heights, from which it has fallen dramatically. A lot of people are having to tighten belts, though the average person in a third-world country would still regard us as overfed and flush with nonessentials and unbelievably wasteful, and they would be right. But our society has become so incredibly wealthy, and our industries have gotten so accomplished at efficiency of production, and our populace has become so addicted to novelty, that our economy has become geared to producing and selling things that, physically speaking, we really don't need, and it supports an advertising industry that exists to convince us that yes, we really *do* need them. Unfortunately, hard times fall hardest on the people who were already poor and hungry. No one should want to see them suffer any more. But as a *culture*, the economic reversals of the past two years would be *beneficial* if they led us to ponder the way our whole society has been plunging into the pile of presents under the tree, ripping off paper and casting the gifts aside after a few seconds' attention, reaching for the next present, disappointed and bewildered and depressed when we come to the end. "Is that all there is?"

The eighth chapter of Deuteronomy is a useful corrective to viewing God as an indulgent super Santa Claus. As the Israelites were finally poised on the edge of the promised land, just about to enter the destination toward which God had been leading them for forty years from the shores of the Red Sea, Moses reminded them of God's steadfast presence and God's dependable provision in the wilderness, and warned of the dangers that would beset their souls in a land of ease and prosperity. All through their long journey, what God had provided was what they had needed—no frills, no excess. Now, God stood ready to discipline them, if necessary, to prevent them from falling into habits of greed and selfishness and idolatry, and keep them what God *intended* them to be—a blessing to the nations.

> Remember the long way that the LORD your God has led you these forty years in the wilderness, in order to humble you, testing you to know what was in your heart, whether or not you would keep his commandments. He *humbled* you by *letting you hunger*, then by feeding you with manna, with which neither you nor your ancestors were acquainted, in order to make you understand that one

"The Good Thing About Hunger"

> does not live by bread alone, but by every word that comes from the mouth of the LORD. (Deut 8:2-3, NRSV)

In forty years, their clothes did not wear out. Their feet did not swell up.

> Know then in your heart that as a *parent* disciplines a *child* so the LORD *your God* disciplines *you*. Therefore keep the commandments of the LORD your God, by walking in his ways and by fearing him. For the LORD your God is bringing you into a good land, a land with flowing streams, with springs and underground waters welling up in valleys and hills, a land of wheat and barley, of vines and fig trees and pomegranates, a land of olive trees and honey, a land where you may eat bread without scarcity, where you will lack nothing, a land whose stones are iron and from whose hills you may mine copper. You shall eat your fill and bless the LORD your God for the good land that he has given you. (Deut 8:5-10, NRSV)

One of the most important things that parents can try to instill in children is a sense of gratitude. I think the moment in each of my children's lives of which I was most proud was the day I first heard them each say "Thank you" to someone and know that they really meant it. Today's culture, largely through the advertising industry, teaches that we have a right to whatever we want (the current interpretation of "the pursuit of happiness"). Me-ism. Materialism. Instant gratification. We get tired of hearing preachers harp on the words. But as the spiritual descendants of the Israelites, as people chosen by God to be bearers of God's promises and witnesses to God's purpose and God's blessing to others, God is counting on you and me to be faithful to God's commandments and to God's truth. Imparting to the next generation a habit of thanksgiving is more difficult now than it has ever been. The reason is that we live in prosperity such as the world has never known. And, so, the danger to our souls, and the souls of our children, has never been so great.

God knew, and Moses realized, how difficult it would be for people living in a prosperous land to remember the *source* of their blessings and to remember the *reason* for their blessings, even, perhaps, to *recognize* their blessings. When we take much for granted, we will be thankful for little. When we forget what we are to do with our prosperity, then it will not be a blessing to others. When we think that it is all ours because of our own industry and intelligence and initiative, or perhaps think that we have received it by right, we assume there is no longer any reason to worship God. This town is filled with SUVs that, on the back, have little fish symbols that say "Truth" gobbling up littler fish symbols that say "Darwin." But the theory of evolution doesn't pose, never *has* posed, nearly the threat to Christian faith that the SUV *itself* symbolizes—a

Thanksgiving

cultural habit of affluence that claims all the world's resources for itself, careless of the effect on other peoples, heedless of the effect on future generations. We have gotten used to eating our fill in a land where we lack nothing. Look around the room. Once upon a time, when our prosperity was less, when the average waistline was narrower, when Christmas gifts were more along the line of a rocking horse and a pair of mittens and some nuts and an orange and a stick of peppermint, sanctuaries were *full* at Thanksgiving. If the preparation for the holiday meal is preventing us from giving thanks to God, then maybe a little hunger would be good for us. And it's not just a matter of the Thanksgiving holiday. It's a matter of the sabbath, too. The issue is that most of us Americans—most of us *Jewish* and *Christian* Americans, even—are too busy with our prosperity to bless the Lord our God for the good land that he has given us. Or is that we, too, have forgotten the source of our blessings?

Paul, while imprisoned in Rome, had received a gift of some sort from the church at Philippi. He had long counted the Philippian Christians as partners in his ministry; they had aided him in many ways, and they continued to do what they could. He began a letter of thanks to them by stating that his imprisonment had actually served to advance the gospel—the whole imperial guard was aware that his imprisonment was because he was being faithful to the Lord Jesus Christ, and other Christians had been emboldened in *their* testimony to the gospel by Paul's example. He seems to have been somewhat embarrassed by their generosity, though—he had long prided himself on not being financially dependent upon anyone, so that no one could criticize the faith on that account, and so that he would always be free to speak the truth to all people. And that prompted him to write something to the Philippians that you and I, used to our warm homes and full plates, might find almost incomprehensible. "I have learned to be content with whatever I have. I know what it is to have little, and I know what it is to have plenty. In any and all circumstances I have learned the secret of being well-fed and of going hungry, of having plenty and of being in need. I can do all things through him who strengthens me" (Phil 4:11b–13, NRSV). And then, so as not to seem ungrateful for what the Philippians had done, he added, "In any case, it was kind of you to share my distress" (Phil 4:14, NRSV).

Paul had had many opportunities to discover something good about hunger and other deprivations—it had all taught him to rely completely upon God, and it had all taught him to be thankful to God for whatever food, clothing, and shelter came his way. He had learned what God first tried to teach his ancestors many centuries before in the wilderness of Sinai, when God humbled them by letting them hunger, and then fed them with manna, with which neither they nor their ancestors were acquainted, in order to make

"The Good Thing About Hunger"

them understand that one does not live by bread alone, but by every word that comes from the mouth of the Lord. And of the kindness of the Philippians, which Paul did not seek and had no reason to claim, but which came as a blessing from God, Paul said, "I have been paid in full and have more than enough" (Phil 4:18a, NRSV). The good thing about hunger is that it teaches us to be thankful for every bite of food. Children will never learn gratitude from parents who give them everything they want. Adults will forget about gratitude if they think they have the right to take everything that they can.

Thanksgiving is a national holiday set aside to do annually as a nation what we should do every day as individuals and at least weekly as congregations—to bless the Lord our God for all the blessings with which we have been blessed, to acknowledge that no person makes it on his or her own, and that no nation is prosperous and successful on its own, but only because *God* gives the soil and the air and the sun and the rain, only because *God* gives the land and the trees and the water and the iron, only because *God* gives the health and the intelligence and the skill—and especially the blessing of generous and merciful love that offers us, all undeserved, the gift of salvation in Jesus Christ. May our lean years help us to remember how greatly we are blessed to have even the barest necessities of life, and teach us to share more freely with those whose material blessings are few. So even hunger may be a blessing from God, a discipline that leads us back to the *source* of *all* our blessings, that reminds us to be *grateful* for *all* our blessings, that teaches us to *share all* our blessings. *That* much hunger would be a *good* thing. Happy Thanksgiving.

Appendix:
"Praying Our Way to San Jose"

In the early summer of 2008, the Presbyterian Church (USA) held a series of worship events at various points along the overland route from Louisville, Kentucky, to the site of the meeting of its General Assembly that year in San Jose, California. Reno, Nevada, was one of the last stops along the route, and Bruce Taylor was invited to preach the sermon for the Reno gathering, based on the San Jose meeting's theme, Micah 6:8.

St. John's Presbyterian Church, Reno, Nevada
JUNE 25, 2008

Micah 6:1–8
1 Timothy 2:1–3
Matthew 7:21–29

"Theme for a Prophetic Church"

As a perpetual member of the Sparks area high school baccalaureate committee, I recently went through the annual process of helping to pick a theme for the celebration that claims graduation from high school as an event of spiri-

Appendix: "Praying Our Way to San Jose"

tual significance. As usual, the themes were suggested without any particular spiritual reflection; it always seems to be a matter of selecting something that sounds good, is slightly *aspirational* if not genuinely *inspirational*, and then I always somehow get assigned the task of finding some scripture passage that supports the theme that has been chosen. As in *past* years, I objected again *this* year that the process is *backwards*; the *theme* should emerge from reflection on the *scriptures*, not the other way around. But once again, I found myself searching a concordance, trying to think of key words that would point me to a few verses from the Bible to give some religious legitimacy to what the committee had already decided the preacher for the occasion should say.

Happily, the theme for the meeting of the General Assembly of the Presbyterian Church (USA) always comes from scripture itself. The challenge in our case is not to allow denominational headlines to force a meaning upon *scripture*, but rather to allow *scripture* to inform and shape the meeting of the General Assembly, and *beyond* the meeting, to shape the program of the church and, derivatively but most importantly, to shape the lives of Presbyterians. Few passages of scripture could be so admirably suited to that last task in *any* season as Micah chapter 6, verse 8: "He has told you, O mortal, what is good; and what does the Lord require of you but to do justice, and to love kindness, and to walk humbly with your God?" (NRSV). The passage from 1 Timothy chosen as the second reading for this series of worship services on the way to San Jose suggests a specific example of how Paul, or somebody writing in his name, thought that should be *done*—prayer of every sort, and for every sort of person. To these two readings I have taken the liberty of adding a third, from the Gospels, believing that every occasion of worship is a proper occasion for hearing the words and remembering the deeds of our Lord (extending the injunction of the *Book of Order*, W-2.2002). The passage that appeared in the lectionary a few Sundays ago is, I think, an important commentary on the apostolic encouragement to prayer, and an explanation of the prophet's critique of Israel's worship life.

The prophets are not known well enough in many of our churches. Despite the insistence of our confessions that the *Old* Testament is every bit as much the concern of Christians as the *New* Testament, some Presbyterians, regrettably, hear from the prophets only around Christmas or when we find some of their verses to be useful in backing up our condemnation of this or that sin. And if that's the only exposure people *have* to the prophets, or the only exposure our people are *given* to the prophets by their *ministers*, the prophetic message and the prophetic task will be misunderstood in our churches. The prophets must have a meaning for us beyond providing ammunition against those with whom we disagree or proof-texting theological claims that

"Theme for a Prophetic Church"

the prophets could not possibly have thought of making. The integrity of the Bible demands that we hear from the books that make up more than a quarter of the Old Testament, and that we hear aright a word that stubbornly insists that the spiritual health of a people is tied directly to the social health of their nation, that the condition of the soul cannot be separated from the treatment of the body, that the well-being of the individual cannot be disconnected from the well-being of the community. And *that* means that the church cannot ignore or isolate itself from the hurts and fears and hunger and hardship of the neediest. The prophets declared that the God who *created* the world and everything that lives in it is supremely *concerned* for the world and everything that lives in it. And nothing in the New Testament contradicts that truth, but only makes it the more emphatic.

Micah emerged from the Judean countryside to lay before people who considered themselves to be God's own the ways in which they were oppressing each other. The rich were oppressing the poor, the rulers were oppressing their subjects, judges were oppressing defendants, employers were oppressing workers, merchants were oppressing their customers. Micah was distressed by the power of urban centers like Jerusalem and Samaria that prospered at the expense of country folk and even the landscape itself. He was disturbed by widows being turned out of their houses and laborers being denied their sabbath rest and debtors being forced into perpetual poverty. He was grieved by religious leaders who were more interested in pleasing their patrons than in honoring God, and who thereby presided over ceremonies and festivals that were hypocritical at best. His rants are sometimes pointed to as evidence against worship that is liturgical or ceremonies that are ritualistic. But Micah's complaints were not against *liturgy* and *ritual* in the *worship place*, but against the behavior of the people *outside* the sanctuary that made *any* worship by them unpleasing to God. If they could not get along with each other, if they dealt dishonestly with each other, if they slandered each other, if they tried to gain advantage over each other, and if they claimed divine sanction for the injuries that they were inflicting on each other, then their worship was untrue and their prayers were inauthentic. They were just spouting so many words, a lot of "Lord, Lord's," even as they wondered why their society was not morally strong enough to ward off the Assyrians and Babylonians at the gates. Burnt offerings could not make up for cold hearts. Thousands of rams could not atone for thousands of hungry and homeless. Ten thousands of rivers of oil were no substitute for justice rolling down like waters. An offering of one's firstborn could not answer for the sin of creating a generation of orphans by gratuitous warfare that betrayed the nation's ultimate trust in soldiers and weapons.

Appendix: "Praying Our Way to San Jose"

"He has told you, O mortal, what is good; and what does the LORD require of you but to do justice, and to love kindness, and to walk humbly with your God" (Mic 6:8, NRSV)? Nations and *leaders* of nations have a hard time doing that. Political rivals would accuse any governor or king or prime minister or president who practiced or advocated living by such a rule as "weak" and "cowardly." Churches, too, have a hard time doing what Micah prescribed, especially when they become enmeshed in the cultural web of consumerism and individualism and nationalism and politicization of questions that are, at root, moral. And if the *church* can't learn or gives up on doing justice and loving kindness and walking humbly with its God, what hope is there that society at *large* will ever *try* it? In the prevailing political and social climate, we could easily be *twice* our current membership if we were less concerned with being faithful to the God who is honored by justice and kindness and humility—if we would simply bless the prevailing culture rather than offering an alternative to it.

An interesting thought occurred to me as I reflected on the honor of having been invited to preach at this waystation along the pilgrimage to San Jose for the renewing of our covenant, as Presbyterians, with each other and with God. At age fifty-seven, I have been a Presbyterian for more than a quarter of the history of our denomination. Does that mean that *I* am that *old*, or that our *church* is that *young*? Here in the year of our Lord 2008, we are easily within three lifespans of John Witherspoon gaveling to order that first meeting of the General Assembly of the Presbyterian Church in the United States of America.

I don't know what was *prayed for* that day, but I *do* know what John Witherspoon *preached* about: the text for the sermon was 1 Corinthians 3:7, reading, in the Authorized Version, as yet uncorrected for its gender-specific pronouns, "So then neither is he that planteth any thing, neither he that watereth; but God that giveth the increase." The Presbyterian Church in the United States of America was born with a summons to spiritual humility ringing in its ears. Two hundred nineteen years later, we still need to be spiritually humble, and to do justice, and to love kindness. And we don't seem always to be doing it—in our congregations, where we are anxious that other churches, less theologically rigorous, are growing faster than *we* are, and in our denominational life, where factions bent on winning a point seem no longer to believe that we are each God's gift to one another.

But we *are* God's gift to one another. And so we must not approach the meeting in San Jose as if we were riding into battle against our opponents who are so obviously deaf to the whisperings or shoutings of the Holy Spirit, eager to defend God against libertinism, on the one hand, or Pharisaism, on the other. Arrogance, pride, triumphalism, vindictiveness, privilege, advantage—those

"Theme for a Prophetic Church"

are the ways of the world which, if we engage in *any* of them, will cause our worship tonight to be rejected by God, which will cause Christ to deny even knowing us, but to be identified by him instead as evildoers even while we claim to be doing his will.

The Task Force on the Peace, Unity, and Purity of the Church accomplished something, or rather *discovered* something, truly amazing a couple of years ago: that when you worship with other people, even those with whom you disagree, when you break bread and drink the cup with other people at the table of reconciliation, even those with whom you disagree, the Lord blesses your efforts. Our church is now embroiled in debate about the recommendations of that Task Force. I happen to be one of those people who applauded their conclusions. But I am also one of those people who thought that the *conclusions* were not nearly as important as the *process*—that regardless of the particular measures that the Task Force unanimously recommended, the Task Force had done Presbyterians and the whole of Christ's church a tremendous benefit by praying with one another, worshiping with one another, listening to one another, and honoring one another. That, I believe, was supremely Christ-like. From what I read in the Bible, God is at least as interested in the way we treat each other in the process of *making* decisions as in the decisions *themselves*. When no one is beyond the scope of our prayers—prayers not that God will defeat them or persuade them to our way of thinking, but that God will bless them and give them peace and preserve their dignity as we are all brought to a better understanding of God's will—then we are walking humbly with our God. When kindness is our method and justice is our passion, then our worship of the God who remembers our frailties and deals with us mercifully, who redeems slaves from oppression and gives them a place in which to grow and prosper, becomes genuine and acceptable to the one to whom all honor is due. Nobody in the scriptures is beyond the possibility of salvation. Therefore, nobody in God's world is beyond the bounds of our concern—a concern which, if we are humbly walking with God, is not a program first to convert or correct, but a compulsion to love and to care for, an insistence that she or he be treated with dignity and justice and kindness, a compassion that makes us advocates for that person before one another and before God. Whenever we forget that truth, whenever we assume an entitlement or presume a privilege, we have turned from the ways of humility, and we risk not walking with God at all.

Will our church be one that models the doing of justice and the loving of kindness and walking humbly with God? We cannot prescribe it for others if we do not practice it ourselves. Will we remember that *others must not* be *coerced* and that *God cannot* be *compelled*? Our task is to plant seeds and to

Appendix: "Praying Our Way to San Jose"

water them, and not to draw attention to ourselves in the doing, but to credit God with the growth and praise God for the bounty. Our righteousness is not capable of being measured in the number of times we sprinkle our conversation with godly talk, but only by the sincerity with which we apply ourselves to lifting up the poor and the powerless, and defending the abused and the outcast, and bending down to heal the wounded and mend the broken. Our salvation is most manifest when we are humble enough that we lose ourselves in the doing. So the theme of the General Assembly at this point in our denominational life *should* be, and the theme of every person who has faith in the God testified to by the prophets *must* be, "Do justice, and love kindness, and walk humbly with God." And it all begins with prayer that excludes none and encompasses all.

List of Sources Cited

Barker, Peter, trans. "Anaweza bwana." In conference booklet, 14. The Hymn Society in the United States and Canada, 1999.
Brueggemann, Walter. *Genesis*. Interpretation: A Bible Commentary for Teaching and Preaching. Atlanta: John Knox, 1982.
Buechner, Frederick. *The Magnificent Defeat*. New York: HarperCollins, 1985.
Buttrick, George A. *The Parables of Jesus*. New York: Harper & Brothers, 1928.
Huston, John, dir. *The African Queen*. Horizon Pictures and Romulus Films Ltd., 1951.
Lowry, Robert. "How Can I Keep from Singing?" In *Glory to God*, edited by David Eicher, 821. Louisville: Westminster John Knox, 2013.
Milton, John. "Paradise Lost: Book V." In *The Works of John Milton, Volume 2, Part 1: Paradise Lost (Book I–XII)—Paradise Regain'd (Book I–IV)*, edited by Frank Allen Patterson, 143–76. New York: Columbia University Press, 1931.
Presbyterian Church (USA). *Book of Occasional Services: A Liturgical Resource Supplementing the Book of Common Worship*. Louisville: Geneva, 1999.
Zeffirelli, Franco, dir. *Jesus of Nazareth*. 1976; ITC Films, 1977.

www.ingramcontent.com/pod-product-compliance
Lightning Source LLC
Chambersburg PA
CBHW051930160426
43198CB00012B/2099